Why Men and Women Act the Way They Do

Bill and Pam Farrel

HARVEST HOUSE PUBLISHERS

EUGENE, OREGON

Published in association with the literary agency of Alive Communications, Inc., 7680 Goddard Street, Ste. #200, Colorado Springs, CO 80920.

Harvest House Publishers and the authors have made every effort to trace the ownership of any copyrighted material used in this book. In the event of a question arising from the use of a quote or humorous sidebar, we encourage anyone holding an unacknowledged copyright to contact the publisher so that proper accreditation can appear in future printings of this book.

Cover by Left Coast Design, Portland, Oregon

Cover illustration by Kreig Barrie

WHY MEN AND WOMEN ACT THE WAY THEY DO
Copyright © 2003 by Bill and Pam Farrel
Published by Harvest House Publishers
Eugene, Oregon 97402
www.harvesthousepublishers.com

Library of Congress Cataloging-in-Publication Data
Farrel, Bill, 1959-
  Why men and women act the way they do / Bill and Pam Farrel.
    p.cm.
Includes bibliographical references.
  ISBN 0-7369-1123-5 (pbk.)
  1. Man-woman relationships—Religious aspects—Christianity. 2. Sex differences—Religious aspects—Christianity. I. Farrel, Pam, 1959- II. Title.
  BT705.8.F37 2003
    305.3—dc21   2003007227

Printed in the United States of America

03 04 05 06 07 08 09 10 11 / BP-MS / 10 9 8 7 6 5 4 3 2 1

Contents

A Note from the Authors

A little girl and a little boy are at day care. The girl approaches the boy and says, "Hey, Tommy, want to play house?"

He says, "Sure! What do you want me to do?"

The girl replies, "I want you to communicate your feelings."

"Communicate my feelings?" said a bewildered Tommy. "I have no idea what that means."

The little girl smirks and says, "Perfect. You can be the husband."

We considered calling this book, *Why Are You and I So Weird?* During our many sessions of counseling couples, we've heard hundreds of people say, "Why did he do that?" "What made her say that?"

In short, the reason is that we're all *different.* We are each a complex blend of characteristics, some of which were determined at our conception as we were each assigned our own unique mix of DNA. Among these genetically received characteristics is the way we look. Our height, our eye and hair color, and the size of our frame can help shape how we think about ourselves—positively or negatively.

Then, as we grew up, other characteristics were added to the mix of who we are through such influences as our family (with all their pluses and minuses), our education, our immediate culture, current events, our geographic environment, the media, and the law.

Many, many things have helped shape us. Knowing what is nature and what is nurture can help us have successful relationships. We must have a grid for determining which things about a coworker, parent, or mate are changeable and which are already determined. In some instances, we are the ones who must adjust, not the other person.

When we wrote *Men Are Like Waffles, Women Are Like Spaghetti*, its study guide, and then the singles version, our research turned up article after article that explained the impact of DNA on each gender. Thousands of pages offered details of how testosterone and estrogen and a host of other hormones affect males and females. As we studied, we saw the inescapable conclusion:

Men and women are different from each other, and therefore, they act differently from one another.

Even more obvious to us, based on our research, is the intelligent design of the human race. The differences in our genders have been placed in us for many good reasons. Men and women are not some cosmic mistake. Our genetic differences are purposeful and can be useful—not just to ourselves but to humankind. We believe God purposefully created these gender differences. By discovering and understanding these differences, we can better reach our own God-given potential and help those we love reach theirs as well.

Our hope is that when you are frustrated with either yourself or a member of the opposite gender, you will remember that the differences that may seem troublesome are, in fact, beneficial. We hope that after reading this book, instead of asking yourself *Why are they so weird?* you will ask, *How can I delight in this difference?* or *How can we use our differences to work for the good of everyone involved?*

We also hope you will have a measure of awe as you discover how "fearfully and wonderfully made" we are. And with the awe, we pray you will also become more understanding. May male readers become a little more compassionate to women in PMS, pregnancy, or perimenopause, and may female readers become a bit more clued in to the impact of testosterone on a male and the unique set of challenges men face as they age.

We also hope this will be a journey of self-discovery. As you learn the part your DNA has contributed to who you are, and as you factor in the cultural, societal, religious, and media influences that have shaped your life, may you discover why you do what you do. And may you also discover what you might want to change. Although DNA determines a lot, it definitely doesn't determine everything!

Enjoy the journey into the male and female mind and the hormonal trek we each make as we try to live life with the DNA cards we are dealt and the choices and opportunities we draw in this game of life. May your journey be filled with insight into why men and women act the way they do.

Pam and Bill Farrel

The pure and simple truth is rarely pure and never simple.
—Oscar Wilde

Why Did You Do That?

Bill remembers…

Pam and I had been enjoying a great evening. We had only been married for about two months, and I was thoroughly enjoying our new life together. We were quietly talking in the living room, reminiscing about our honeymoon and sharing our dreams of the future. I was just about to conclude that my life had never been better—when it happened.

Suddenly Pam's expression went from one of peace to shock. I must have said something frightfully wrong. Pam bolted to her feet and tearfully cried out, "You don't love me anymore!" With that, she ran into our bedroom and *enthusiastically* closed the door behind her. When I anxiously followed her into the bedroom, I found her lying on the bed, sobbing. Being a young husband, I was eager to be supportive, so I went to great lengths to console her and reassure her that my love for her was intact. At the same time, I was asking myself, "Why did she do that?"

Pam remembers…

Later that year, we were sharing our second Christmas together. We were young. We were in love. We were poor. As a result, we decided we would make Christmas presents for our families rather than buy them. Bill decided to build a clock for his parents. He spent many days cutting, building, sanding, and finishing his handiwork. And when the clock was finally ready, Bill triumphantly carried it up the stairs to our apartment and set it in the empty spare bedroom. I was busy with other holiday preparations, so I didn't notice at first that Bill wasn't anywhere to be found. I looked in our bedroom, and he wasn't there. I checked the storage space in the apartment, and he wasn't there. I checked the bathroom, and he wasn't there. Finally, I checked the spare bedroom, where I found Bill sitting and staring at the clock!

"What are you doing?" I asked in utter amazement.

"I'm just admiring my handiwork. What do you think?"

I said, "It looks great. I'm really proud of you," and walked out of the room expecting Bill to follow so we could get on with the rest of the chores on our to-do list. But he didn't follow. He just sat in the room staring at the clock.

Why did he do that?

Living in Amazement

Our middle son, Zachery, loves people and lives for social events. As a result, his first homecoming dance was a big deal for all of us. He was nervous and excited and intent on doing it right. When he discovered that his shirt was missing a button, he mildly panicked. He had learned how to sew buttons on during one of his classes at school, so he set out to solve the problem on his own. After he left, we noticed that the sewing needle he used was stuck in one of the armrests on the loveseat. The thread was propped up on the other armrest. The container that held the buttons was on the couch. The scissors were on the coffee table. The shirt he wore while he put the button on was on the floor of the living room, and his hairbrush was on the woodstove. The forensic evidence of his activities was unmistakable.

Why did he do that?

We have good friends who are missionaries in Bogota, Colombia. They recently visited us in San Diego with Candy, the ten-year-old Colombian girl they are adopting. We decided to take them to a San Diego Padres game. While we were there, we signed Candy up as a member of the Junior Padres Club. As part of the club the kids get a "credit card" that can be inserted into kiosks around the stadium. The machine responds by spitting out coupons and information cards. I (Bill) was walking in the stadium with our youngest son, Caleb, and Candy. Caleb put his card in one of the machines, and it rewarded him with a coupon. Candy thought that was pretty neat and reached for her card. She suddenly realized that she left her card with her dad. The look of panic on her face was something I had never seen on my three boys. Her eyebrows dipped. Her forehead wrinkled. Then tears began to flow. Her voice transformed into a shrieking whine. At first, I thought someone was mortally wounded! Then she said, "I forgot my card. We have to go get my dad right now. I have to put my card in that machine or my day will be *ruined!*"

Why did she do that?

The Hovering Question

The question hovers everywhere in human relationships and takes on many forms. Consider the following variations on the theme.

Questions Women Ask About Men

Why does he roll his eyes every time I tell him we need to coordinate calendars?

Why do men like to burp?

Why does a man ask a woman to spend time with him—and then refuse to talk?

Why did he talk so much when we were dating but then stop talking when we got married?

What is so great about the television?

Why does he spend so much time watching sports?

What's with the violent movies?

Why does he stare at women?

How can he eat that much?

Why does he say mean things?

Why is he so angry?

Does he have to win everything?

Why won't he ask for directions?

Why does he ignore important issues in his life?

Why does he blame me for his struggles?

Why won't he stand up for himself?

Questions Men Ask About Women

Why is she so emotional?

Why do women spend so much time on how they look?

Why do women go to the bathroom in groups?

How can she talk so much?

Why can't she let things go?

How can everything be that important to her?

Why do her friends' opinions mean so much to her?

Are they all this sensitive?

How can they be so nice and so difficult at the same time?

Why do they work so hard at relationships?

Simply Irresistible

Why do men and women act the way they do? The question is simple, but finding the answer can drive you crazy. The simplest answer is that men act like men and women like women because they are fundamentally different in genetic and chemical makeup. This is true in the same sense that spiders weave webs and snowflakes fall to the ground. Every spider web is a spider web, but each of them is a work of art. Every snowflake is a snowflake, but each of them is uniquely designed.

The answer becomes more complicated when we remember that each of us acts as an individual with a unique set of characteristics and life experiences. Therefore, no one answer can explain our behavior without exception. A simple statement based on genetics does not account for the individual. A complicated paradigm that accounts for all of a person's experiences would be impossibly cumbersome.

In this book we will look at the question in practical terms. Your life is a journey. You have traveled many paths that combine to make you the unique person you are today. Some of the paths you did not choose. You did not choose to be male or female. You weren't given the opportunity to choose your dad and mom. You weren't asked when in the history of the world you would like to appear. You were given these paths to walk. Your only choice is to walk them well or to complain about them.

Other paths you walk by your own choosing. You can decide to be married or single. You can decide where you want to live. You can set goals for yourself and choose your friends. You can direct your internal attitudes and screen your entertainment options. Because no two people walk the same paths, everyone is unique.

I (Bill) was at a gathering the other day with about a hundred people, and I noticed some of their similarities and differences.

Peter was impressive in his appearance and forceful in his words. He obviously expected everyone in the room to agree with him and to be impressed with him.

Brent was on the other end of the spectrum. He was physically unattractive and spoke awkwardly. People tried to be patient, but he was so slow in putting his words together that his listeners finished his thoughts for him. He was intelligent, but few people benefited from his knowledge because they couldn't stand to wait for the information. He was, however, attractively humble because he couldn't rely on his own ability to impress people.

Susan giggled at everything. I don't know if she was nervous or if she thought being squeaky was cute, but she didn't stop. At one point, someone confided that a close friend had passed away the previous week, and she started laughing!

Judy probably wanted to go unnoticed but was so obvious in her dowdy appearance that everyone saw her. Her pants were about twenty years out of date. Her blouse would have looked better on someone twice her age. Her hair was plain, her makeup was missing, and her beauty was hidden.

Then there was the chatterbox. Danette believed that everything about her life was fascinating to everyone. She described the entire process of how she chose her outfit for the day. She relived her birthday party, her vacation, and the previous Christmas with her family. Every detail was spelled out in vivid descriptions.

Janet, on the other hand, was truly impressive. She had obviously digested huge amounts of information about modern culture and could synthesize it in confident and concise statements. She elicited confidence in those around her as she shared opinions about the most important issues of the day with calm assurance.

What Did You Say?

The interaction between these people was entertaining to say the least. Peter, of course, began the conversation. "What we need is a strong leader. Someone who will lead the way without worrying about stepping on people's toes."

"Well..." droned Brent, "I think...a good...leader...cares..."

"You mean he cares about people's feelings," snapped Peter. "I think too much is made of that today. You just can't trust feelings."

Just then Susan walked up and said, "Are you guys talking about feelings? I don't know why but I think that's funny." With that she broke out in a subdued giggle that made Peter roll his eyes in disgust. Susan could tell Peter wasn't interested, so she quickly turned her head and walked to the group where Judy was standing.

"Judy," she giggled, "what do you think of my new outfit?"

Judy looked her over with disinterest and said, "It's nice, but wasn't it pretty expensive? I buy most of my clothes at the thrift store. It is amazing what good clothes people get rid of. I think my outfit only cost me two dollars."

At that Danette took over. "I was going to wear my red outfit today, but I thought it probably wasn't the right time of year for that. I will probably bring it out closer to Christmas. So I decided that the best thing for tonight was probably jeans and a button-down blouse since I knew we would be outside tonight and the weather is just starting to get nippy. So I pulled out my blue jeans and my black jeans and laid them out on my bed. Then I took out all my button-down blouses. I have eight of them. It took a little while, but I finally narrowed it down to either the white one or the pink one. The white one looked best with the blue jeans and the pink one looked best with the black ones. I had the hardest time deciding, but then I realized I was in a black jeans sort of mood and the rest, as they say, is history."

At that point I turned to see another group deep in discussion with Janet. "The upcoming election is going to be one of the most critical I have seen. The new governor will appoint three Supreme Court justices, and that could change the entire flow of the judicial branch. I have been working with a group of concerned citizens who are trying to get the word out. If you know of anyone who would like to help, please let me know."

The Strange Paradox

The more I took notice of all that was going on around me, the more I came to realize that everyone in the room was unique. They all had common features, but they were amazingly different from each other. They had unique talents, voices, personalities, and interests. The similar ingredients of our lives have been mixed together in a way that makes each of us one of a kind.

We are all human, and yet we are all unique. There has never been, and will never be, anyone exactly like you. You have much in common with other people, but no one looks exactly like you or acts exactly like you or makes decisions exactly like you. As a result, there is no easy answer to the question, "Why do men and women act the way they do?"

The First Step on the Journey

The journey of discovering why you act the way you do begins with your gender. The fact that you are male or female determines the raw material you have to work with. In our book *Men Are Like Waffles, Women Are Like Spaghetti* we summarize the differences between men and women.

Men are like waffles. By this statement we do not mean that men "waffle" on their decisions and are generally unstable. What we mean is that men process life in boxes. If you look at a waffle, you see a collection of boxes separated by walls. The boxes are all separate from each other and make convenient holding places. That is typically how a man processes life. His thinking is divided up into boxes that have room for one issue and one issue only. The first issue of life goes in the first box, the second goes in the second box, and so on. The typical man then spends time in one box at a time and one box only. When a man is at work, he is at work. When he is in the garage tinkering around, he is in the garage tinkering. When he is watching TV, he is simply watching TV. That is why he looks as if he is in a trance and he can ignore everything else going on around him. Social scientists call this *compartmentalizing*—putting life and responsibilities into different compartments.

As a result of living life in boxes, men are natural problem solvers. They enter a box, size up the problem, and formulate a solution. In their careers, they consider how to be successful and focus on that. In communication, they look for the bottom line and get there as quick as possible. In decision making, they look for the approach they can buy into and apply it as often as possible.

A man will strategically organize his life in boxes and then spend most of his time in the boxes he can succeed in. This is such a strong motivation that he will seek out the boxes that work for him and ignore the boxes that confuse him or make him feel like a failure. For instance, a man whose career holds the possibility of success will spend more and more time at work at the expense of other priorities. On the other hand, a man who always falls short at work or feels he never meets the expectations around him may find out that he is pretty good at being lazy. He will then develop a commitment to being lazy because he knows he can do that well.

Women are like spaghetti. In contrast to men's waffle-like approach, women process life as if it were a plate of spaghetti. A plate of spaghetti has individual noodles that all touch one another. Each noodle intersects a lot of other noodles, and following one leads you to others seamlessly. That is how women face life. Every thought and issue is connected to every other thought and issue in some way. Life is much more of a process for women than it is for men.

This is why a woman is typically better at multitasking than a man. She can talk on the phone, prepare a meal, make a shopping list, work on the planning for tomorrow's business meeting, give instructions to her children as they are going out to play, and close the door with her foot—without skipping a beat. Since all her thoughts, emotions, and convictions are connected, she is able to process more information and keep track of more activities.

As a result, most women are trying to connect life together. They solve problems much differently than men do. For women to quickly solve a problem when the issues involved are disconnected from each other is an act of denial. And so, women consistently need to talk things through. In conversation, they can link together the logical, emotional, relational, and spiritual aspects of an issue. The links come to them naturally so that the conversation is effortless. If they are able to connect all the issues together, the answer to the question at hand bubbles to the surface and is readily accepted.

Physically Fit

Our identities as men and women begin with our biology. The nucleus of every cell in the human body has 46 chromosomes that determine our physical features. These 46 chromosomes are made up of 23 matched pairs. Every aspect of your physical makeup, including hair color, eye color, height, and the functioning of your internal organs, is determined by these combinations of chromosomes.

One set of these chromosomes is different from the other 22 pairs. In women, the two chromosomes are relatively long and resemble each other. These are called *X chromosomes*. In men, one of the chromosomes is long, but the other is very short. The short chromosome is referred to as the *Y chromosome*. Simply put, if you have a Y chromosome you develop as a male, and if you do not have a Y chromosome you develop as a female.

The easiest way to explain the physical difference is to go back to the waffles and spaghetti picture. Both of these items begin with wheat flour but become very different as ingredients are added and the food is prepared. In the same way, apart from a DNA test, you cannot tell the sex of an embryo at the onset of pregnancy. Sometime during the second month of pregnancy, a signal begins the male developmental process. Only the Y chromosome responds to this signal, so a female embryo ignores the signal while a male embryo begins a flurry of activity.

This signal specifically impacts the developing gonad. In a male, the gonad becomes the testis, while in a female it becomes an ovary. "All the other sex differences, in genitalia, body size, muscles, liver, brain, body chemistry, and behavior, come about by the influence of the testis or ovary on the remainder of the body, an influence which takes no account of the genetic sex of the body cells."[2] In other words, testosterone and estrogen have a profound influence on every aspect of our lives.

The Male Interruption

The human embryo is programmed to become a female and will only develop into a male if it is interrupted by a swing in the male direction. In other words, left unchecked, every embryo will be female.

As a result, the fetal development of a little girl is a much calmer process than that of a little boy.

Hormones cause an intense interruption process in a male embryo. Even before the boy can say a word, he is bombarded with messages. A developmental assault team assembles within him to block and redirect his life.

Central Command sends out the orders, "Stop all development of the female genitals."

The supply staff is ordered, "Turn on the juice. Fill the armory with testosterone and androgens."

The first torpedo gets loaded and released at about two months. It explodes upon the boy's world and begins a six-week assault that surrounds him in a testosterone bath that rocks his world. Certain connections between the two sides of his brain are severed, and others are prevented from developing. Other portions of his brain are sent into hyperdrive. New links called *androgen receptors* are established, allowing the free flow of male hormones to reach their targets.

At roughly 14 weeks, the level of testosterone in the male fetus is about as high as it will be during puberty. But then suddenly the assault is called off, and hormone levels drop to very low levels. A break in the action gives the boy a chance to rest for a few weeks. Just before birth, however, another six-month assault begins, reaching a second peak at about the age of two months. This is another preparation stage when certain parts of his body are made ready to receive the signals during puberty that will make him bigger and stronger than his female friends.

Outside Influences

Many attempts have been made over the years to explain away the differences between men and women as simply the result of cultural training. We are told that we act the way we do only because we have been taught to do so by our parents, educators, and the media. Indeed, many of the differences can be attributed to the influence of the culture we live in, but the whole truth is more complicated than that. Genetics and the environment combine to create results like these:

- In one study, college students played with a baby who was either introduced as Johnny or Jenny or was not identified by name or gender. Observers provided three toys: a doll, a football, and a teething ring. People were more likely to hand Johnny the football, the unidentified child received the doll a bit more often, and Jenny was handed the doll five times as often as the football.

- Another study discovered that boys' rooms had a total of 375 vehicles *each,* and girls' rooms had 7!

- Parents decorate boy's and girls' bedrooms differently. In one study, researchers visited children's rooms who were ages one to six. The boys' rooms were typically decorated with animal themes, and the girls' rooms were more likely to have flowers, fringes, and ruffles.

- Parents are also more likely to call their baby girls by terms of affection like "honey," "sweetie," and "angel," and they are more likely to play vigorously with sons than with daughters.

- Parents encourage boys to be more independent than their female counterparts. For example, boys are left alone in a room at a younger age and allowed to cross a street at an earlier age.

- Fathers are more likely than mothers to stress femininity in their daughters and stereotypically masculine dress, toys, and behavior in their sons.

- Parents are more tolerant of aggressive behavior in sons than in their daughters.

- Hasbro toys tried to accommodate feminists by creating a dollhouse that both girls and boys would be attracted to.

However, when testing it, the designers found that girls played with the dollhouse by moving furniture around, dressing up dolls, and putting them in the house, while the boys launched baby carriages off the dollhouse roof![4]

Family Ties

If your gender determines the first path you must walk on the journey of your life, then your family determines the second. These are the two most powerful influences on your life during your most formative years. They profoundly affect the way you define yourself, the skills you have to work with, and the way you interpret your environment.

Families are like herds of wild horses. The family you grew up in is a collection of fully alive, energetic, and influential individuals. Some people come into the family system wild-eyed and full of fire. They believe from the beginning of their lives that they should be in charge. They challenge everything and seek to control everything that affects their lives. Other individuals come into their family full of adventure and playful energy. They are always seeking for something new and are consistently wandering off as they explore their world. They do not challenge those in charge, but they can be hard to keep track of. Still others have a compliant, easygoing spirit and are content to follow the herd. They naturally obey and are pleased to let others lead.

Because each new member of the family comes in as a "wild horse," families simply run by instinct unless they bridle the energy of the family and deliberately channel it. Many people grew up in a "wild" family that simply ran by instinct. Sometimes the instinct of the family is very positive, but more often than not, the family that runs wild creates insecure individuals who must live with the scars of growing up in an untamed environment.

Both of us grew up in families that loved us deeply but ran on instinct. I (Bill) grew up in a home with a dad who was extremely nice and a mom with a strong personality who was afraid of many things. She planned her life around her fear. She controlled every situation, questioned every decision, and isolated us from outside influences. In her fear, she bombarded my sister, brother, and myself with statements such as, "You don't have what it takes. You will never be anything. You are never going to be truly successful in your life." These statements were mingled with anger, long lectures, and stifling demands. I am convinced my mom meant well, but the mixture of affection with these negative statements created a strange behavior pattern in my life.

When I was a teen, I decided to prove my mom wrong. I committed myself to showing her and everyone else that I could make something of myself. I earned good grades and disciplined myself in sports, thinking I could be a college athlete and get a great education. What a lousy motivation! No one wants his mom to be wrong, and the energy required to fulfill a plan like this is exhausting. I was too hard on myself, and so I underachieved. I developed a pattern of *almost*. I was *almost* successful in many things, but I could never seem to finish the course. Needless to say, I didn't play college sports, I didn't get a scholarship, and I didn't really understand why.

I fell in love with Pam because she is outgoing and passionate about life. She can squeeze more out of every minute in life than anyone else I know. She is caring, compassionate, positive, and energetic!

I (Pam) grew up with a father who loves me more than anyone, but who has a pain deep in his heart that he chose to answer with alcohol. As a result, I grew up with Dr. Jekyll and Mr. Hyde. When my dad wasn't drinking, he was a wonderful father who lavished me with praise. He was fun loving and spent lots of time with me and my friends. He has a great sense of humor and is fiercely loyal to me. But when he was drinking, he would turn angry and unreasonable. He transformed into a distant, demanding, unrelenting parent. Nothing was good enough for him, and I could never figure out how to please him. As a result of this double-sided relationship with my dad, I have struggled with a general mistrust of all men, a huge fear of rejection, and fear of failure.

Late in our teen years, Bill and I both heard that men tend to marry women like their moms and women tend to marry men like their dads. It is impossible to explain the frightening impact this statement had on each of us. It is equally impossible to explain the deep sense of relief we have experienced as we discovered that this is a general trend and not a universal law. We cannot help but bring these experiences into our marriage and family, but they do not have to define the rest of our lives. Couples can choose what to do with the scars of growing up in a "wild" environment.

Bridle the Horses

Other people, however, have grown up in healthy, well-balanced homes. Their parents recognized the true nature of each member of the family and guided the process of growth in their lives. Because their parents deliberately directed the family, these people are confidently productive and pursue their purpose with clarity and focus.

Jeremy is a friend of ours who grew up this way. His dad was a successful businessman who balanced the demands of his career with a strong commitment to family. He was reasonable in his discipline and inspiring in his motivation. Jeremy's mom, likewise, was a steady and supportive parent. She prayed regularly with all of her children, supported them in their pursuits, and guided them as they did their own problem solving. Jeremy figured out early in life that he wanted to be a doctor who took time each year to travel to a foreign country to help the underprivileged.

He met Susan in college. She also grew up in a home with supportive parents who gave clear messages and consistent applause for her accomplishments. She is now a nurse who accompanies her husband to these foreign countries. She volunteers in her community, has a strong network of friends, and is generally relaxed in the midst of her productivity. Jeremy and Susan have a hard time understanding the struggles of their friends who grew up in dysfunctional homes. They are sensitive and caring people, but they have no context for sensing what it is like to grow up in a family that is anything other than supportive.

The Experience of You

Your gender and your family are, by far, the greatest influences in your life. But you are not just the product of your genes and your family style. You have had a unique collection of experiences and decisions that add to your life and shape your attitudes. These events have greatly influenced your understanding of who you are and how you should relate to the people in your life. You have embraced a collection of ideas and beliefs that guide you in your journey. For this reason, the story of your life is very important, and any event in your life provides an opportunity to learn and grow.

For instance, we were recently in Wisconsin in the month of February. The high temperature while we were there was 2 degrees! For some people, this would not be a big deal, but we live in San Diego County where the temperature was 72 degrees. I (Bill) was frozen, but I noticed that the natives to the area were moving at a very normal pace.

I asked one of the men, "How do you do this?"

"How do we do what?" he asked.

"How do you live in such a cold place?"

"We just learn to adapt and keep up as normal a pace as possible. Sometimes we get some pretty hard lessons. A few years ago, I went camping with two friends when it was like this outside. We each took our own tents, but I was the only one with a heater. We weren't afraid of freezing because we all had sleeping bags that were designed for extreme cold, but we still had a lot to learn. Because I had the heater, we all met in my tent to play cards and visit before going to sleep. Eventually, my friends went to their own tents, and we all climbed in our sleeping bags. I turned off the heater and slept very peacefully. It never occurred to any of us that the warm tent with the cold outside was forming condensation on the outside of the tent. In the morning, we woke up, and I discovered that the condensation had frozen solid. We couldn't fold up the tent! We knew the tent wouldn't thaw out until April, so we just drove off and left it! It was a tough lesson, but we learned that we just have to adjust."

Adjusting—that is what this book is about. We must remember that life is a journey. The paths of this journey will be filled with educational experiences, media input, technological advances, and significant relationships. As you adjust to each of these influences, you will add to the story of your unique journey.

The History Channel

The discussion of why men and women act the way they do is nothing new. People have been asking this question since the Garden. The facts about testosterone and estrogen have not changed, but the way we adapt to our environment has been changing throughout history. At other times in history, our understanding of life remained rather static. People held the same views for generations. But throughout history, key events have adjusted the lens through which we look at life. Women's suffrage, World War II, the civil rights movement, the birth control pill, and the personal computer have all deeply affected the way we operate in this world.

Throughout this book we will be taking a journey—a journey of information and insight as we explore the various factors that make us who we are. The discussion is a fascinating and complex venture that we will never completely understand or explain. At the same time, the issues are so intertwined in our daily lives that we are forced to think about them, talk about them, agonize over them, and live out our conclusions. At the end of each chapter, we offer questions to help you participate in the discussion. They make great conversation starters for couples or small groups. Enjoy the dialogue, and welcome to the journey!

> A friend asked a gentleman why he never married. Replied the gentleman, "Well, I guess I just never met the right woman."

"Oh, come on now," said the friend. "Surely you have met at least one girl that you wanted to marry."

"Yes, there was a girl...once. She was the one perfect girl—the only perfect girl I really ever met. She was just the right everything...the one for me."

"Well, why didn't you marry her?" asked the friend.

"She was looking for the perfect man."

Why Did You Do That?

1. What did you learn about men? About women?

2. What does being a man mean to you? What does being a woman mean to you?

3. What toys do you buy for little boys? For little girls?

4. Do you think our identity is determined mostly by nature (our DNA) or nurture (our environment)?

5. What are some differences you notice between the genders? Do you think men and women work differently, think differently, and relate differently?

6. In what ways do you think men and women are similar?

Those who can't think, fight.

—JUDY ROBINSON
Lost in Space

The Male and Female Brains

"Grad Nite" is a big deal at our sons' high school. The event begins at 10 P.M. on the night of graduation and ends at 5 A.M. the next morning. The gymnasium is decorated in a particular theme. This year, the theme was "Cruisin' into the Knight." The entrance to the gym was decorated like an ocean wharf and featured a 48-foot-long, 12-foot-high cruise ship. Beyond the ship was a ballroom, a casino room, and an indoor island with a volcano, a pirate ship, and a treasure store. In a separate room, "The Caribbean Café" provided all-night ice cream, air hockey tables, a temporary-tattoo booth, and dance machines. In the courtyard in front of the gym entrance was "The MidKnight Café," serving a variety of food all night long. The parking lot was transformed into a carnival of games that included bungee trampolines, rock climbing walls, and laser tag. The purpose of the event was to create a collection of memories that the students could never again experience at one time. As the event committee made plans and preparations, the differences between men and women were consistently on display.

Light the Torches

On the last day of preparation, the committee debated about tiki torches. Two men thought that tiki torches on the front of the building would look awesome. The torches were mounted so that they were at least four feet away from any structure. Making fire a part of Grad Nite gave the men a tremendous sense of accomplishment. But then some women surveyed the situation. The ceiling of the food court was a blue plastic tarp. Some of the torches were directly in front of the tarp even though they were four feet above it. The close proximity made the women nervous, so they began to lobby for those torches to remain unlit.

The battle raged for about two hours. The men thought the women were being overly cautious and responded, "That's ridiculous...humph—haven't they ever seen tiki torches in Hawaii?" The women responded just as passionately, "You guys are being reckless. Safety comes first. What if the tarp catches fire? How will you feel then?"

The committee decided to light the torches in the afternoon to see if they were indeed safe. The torches burned for an hour and a half. During that time, the women walked around, eyeing the situation, looking for potential disaster. The men walked by, took a quick look, noticed no tarp was on fire, and walked triumphantly on to the next task. Finally the women humbly admitted that the men were right but asked that a fire extinguisher be placed nearby just in case. One of the men found a fire extinguisher and placed it in the food court saying, "You won't need this, but here it is anyway."

The men's and women's responses to the situation were interesting. The men had a new swagger in their walks. They were *right*. They had proven their point, and they felt good about their victory. The women, on the other hand, seemed okay with the fact that the men had been right. They had pushed the men to prove that the idea was safe, and they were content to let the men think they had won.

Think About It

Men and women are incredible beings. Our bodies are made up of complex systems that interrelate to create a functioning organism. We breathe, we eat, we create, we get sick, we heal. Twenty-four hours per day, seven days per week, our bodies work to carry on the process of life. Physically, men and women have more similarities than differences. We all have respiratory systems, digestive systems, bloodstreams, and the like. At the same time, we have many differences. Researcher Simon LeVay says, "The three most significant areas of sexual differentiation involve the internal genitalia, the external genitalia, and the brain."[1]

In other words, we think differently from each other, and those different ways of processing life make for some interesting situations. In the movie *Indiana Jones and the Last Crusade*, Dr. Jones and a German agent named Elsa argue about who should be in charge and whose way of doing things is best. Indiana Jones settles the issue with the following statement: "Listen. Since I've met you, I've nearly been incinerated, drowned, shot, and chopped into fish bait. We're caught in the middle of something sinister here. My guess is Dad found out more than he was looking for, and until I'm sure, I'm going to continue to do things the way I think they should be done." We often feel this way in the battle of the sexes. Our relationships are risky, irritating, and irresistible. We are fascinated and frustrated with one another at the same time.

Using Your Head

The structure and operation of the brain are fascinating. The three main parts of the brain are the cerebrum, the cerebellum, and the brain stem. The cerebrum is the largest part of the brain, with left and right hemispheres. The cerebrum is the structure most of us think about when we hear the word *brain*. It is pink and spongy with lots of wrinkles in it. Most of the functions of the brain are contained in the cerebrum. The cerebellum is a relatively small portion of the brain located immediately behind the brain stem. It fine-tunes our motor activity and movements. The cerebellum gives us the ability to write, raise a fork to our mouth, sew, drive, type on a keyboard, and turn the pages of a book. The brain stem is located at the lower portion of the brain and connects the brain to the spinal cord.

Between the cerebrum and the brain stem are three structures—the thalamus, the hypothalamus, and the pituitary gland—that help us function normally. The thalamus relays sensory information to the cerebrum, enabling us to see, hear, and smell. The hypothalamus helps regulate body functions such as thirst and appetite, as well as sleep, aggression, and sexual behavior. It handles information from the autonomic nervous system and sends messages to the pituitary gland. The pituitary gland produces hormones that play a role in growth, development, and various other physiological variables.

Thinking Begins in the Womb

The gonad in the developing fetus has a profound impact on the brain. As pointed out in chapter 1, the gonad will develop as a female unless it is interrupted by the presence of the gene that triggers male development. The gonad's development as male or female determines whether certain parts of the brain become more electrically alive or less active. It can cause certain synaptic connections to form or to instruct other parts of the brain to synthesize certain chemicals. "Steroids can even control whether brain cells live or die."[2]

The complex structure of the brain provides limitless possibilities of how the brain can work. The average human brain contains about 10 billion nerve cells called neurons. Connecting these nerve cells are approximately 10 trillion synapses. The sheer numbers of cells and connections give the brain the potential for an inexhaustible and sophisticated network of connectivity and productivity.

However, the brain is not nearly as efficient as it could be. The great majority of all the connections (synapses) in the brain are made with neurons that are close by. This is not to say that long-distance connections do not exist, but most of them are local calls. In addition, each neuron, on average, can only be connected with 1,000 of the 10 billion nerve cells in the brain. This means that the brain is vastly under connected and relatively inefficient. The way these connections are made and the particular connections that are most active deeply affect the way the brain works and the way each individual perceives the world. As it turns out, the male and female brains make different connections.

The maleness or femaleness of the brain appears to be determined during fetal and early postnatal development. Understandably, experiments have not been done with human beings to determine the effects of hormones early in life, but many experiments have been done with rats because of their similar physiology. Male rat pups who are castrated either prior to birth or immediately after birth and then allowed to grow up will not demonstrate male-typical sexual behavior. This holds true even if they are given testosterone during their adult years. These same rats will, in fact, demonstrate female-typical sexual behavior if they are given estrogen and progesterone as adults. If, however, castration is not performed until a few days after birth, neither of these effects takes place. Given testosterone, they portray male typical behavior. If they are given estrogen and progesterone, they fail to display female typical behavior. This is significant evidence that the time around birth is critical for the development of the brain and the signals it will send out for the rest of life. Much of a brain's maleness is tied to the peak in testosterone that happens from birth to about six months of age.[3]

Get Connected

Many differences in the brains of men and women go well beyond sexual behavior. Most obvious among the differences is the fact that, on average, men's brains are approximately 15 percent larger than women's brains. But size is certainly not everything! The way the connections in the brain are organized determines men and women's behavior much more than the size of the brain.

For instance, part of the hypothalamus—the medial preoptic area—is highly influenced by androgens, which are present in much larger doses in males than in females. At least one nucleus in this portion of the brain is larger in men and is interconnected according to a uniquely male plan. "Electron microscopic studies of the area have revealed differences between male and female rats in the shape and position of synapses made between neurons, and second, immunohistochemistry has shown sex differences in the distribution of several neurotransmitters in the region."[4]

Female-typical sexual behavior, however, is influenced by an area in the brain a few millimeters behind the medial preoptic area. This area is called the ventromedial nucleus. It is relatively large as nuclei go in the region and impacts functions other than sexual behavior. Interestingly, this region of the brain regulates eating behavior in women, and damage to this area can cause obesity.

It seems fair, then, to ask, what would have happened if the three wise men had been three wise women? The answer is, they would have asked directions, arrived on time, cleaned the stable, and made a casserole. Why? Because their thinking is organized differently.

Information Superhighway

A region of the brain called the corpus callosum provides a fascinating distinction between men and women. "The corpus callosum is the major connection between the left and right hemispheres of the cerebral cortex."[5] In other words, it is the information superhighway in the brain. This region acts as a bridge as the two hemispheres of the brain send signals back and forth. Between the two hemispheres is a fluid-filled gap that houses the neurons that connect the two halves. Related to the corpus callosum is a structure called the anterior commissure. A smaller version of the corpus callosum, it resides further back in the cerebral cortex and serves a similar function of transporting messages from one side of the brain to the other. Both the corpus callosum and the anterior commissure are larger in women than in men. This means that the two sides of the brain are more connected in women than in men.

For years, people have readily accepted that women generally integrate the issues of their lives more effectively than men do. They have an innate ability to see the relationships between the various areas of their lives and to connect them together in conversation, planning, and decision making. Rather than separating everything into individual components of life, they can make a unified whole out of the parts. Women's brains appear to be better equipped for this type of activity than men's. This has a fascinating application to verbal skills. The back part of the corpus callosum is called the splenium and holds the connections that are related to visual and verbal functioning. In general, women are more adept at speech, and they are more capable of using both sides of their brains in conversation. "In fact, Melissa Hines and her colleagues at UCLA have reported that, among normal women, those who score the best on tests of verbal fluency also tend to have the largest splenium of the corpus callosum."[6]

Why Am I Hungry?

Men and women's brains respond differently to being hungry and full. A report in the June 2002 issue of the *American Journal of Clinical Nutrition* posts some interesting differences in the way men and women process hunger and eating.

- When hungry, men had more activity than women did in the paralimbic region of the brain, an area involved in processing emotion.

- When hunger was satisfied, women had more activity than men did in the occipital cortex, the seat of vision.

- When hunger was satisfied, men had more activity than women did in an area of the prefrontal cortex associated with feelings of satisfaction.[7]

This study suggests that men feel better about eating than women do. They experience a more rewarding feeling and generally feel more satisfied with food in their stomachs. The expression, "The way to a man's heart is through his stomach" may actually be based on activity in the brain. Eating causes activity in the area of the brain that produces satisfying emotions for men. In the same way, hunger causes emotional reactions in men much more than in women.

This was played out in an episode of the TV show *Home Improvement*. Tim was trying to improve his relationship with his wife, Jill. She was upset with him because he wasn't taking the emotions of their relationship seriously. He decided to devote an episode of *Tool Time* to the topic of men getting in touch with their feelings. He called two burly men to the front and sat them on stools. He then asked, "How do you feel?"

The first man thought for a minute and replied, "I feel hungry."

The second man said, "Now that you mention it, I feel hungry too."

The first one then interrupted, "And now that I feel hungry, I am feeling angry. I need to get some food."

With that, the two men dismissed themselves from the show and headed out on the hunt for something to eat. We had a great time laughing about the show, but evidence now suggests that a man's emotional state and his level of hunger are intricately tied together in his brain.

Raising three sons has given us an eyewitness view of this phenomenon. The first thing our kids say when they get home is, "I'm hungry!" When we ask them how they are doing, they commonly answer, "I'm hungry." Some of the greatest times we have had as a family are around the dinner table because their moods change with a good meal. When our middle son, Zachery, was young, he would get angry if he hadn't eaten for a while. At first, we thought this was a behavior problem, but then we noticed that his anger disappeared as soon as he ate. We learned early in his life to feed him before we talked about his behavior. We suspect we will need to fill in his wife about this need!

Women love to eat also, but they respond differently. Eating stimulates the area of a woman's brain that influences sight. In short, they can see better and become more aware of their environment during a meal. The fascinating possibility is that the area of the brain that sharpens sight appears to be closely linked to the region of the brain that stimulates conversation. No wonder that men and women like to meet around the dinner table! The men are grumpy until they get food in their stomachs, and then they feel loved when they eat. They are generally more content and willing to listen in a relaxed environment. At the same time, food sharpens the senses of women and stimulates topics for conversation. A great meal really does make everyone happier!

Keeper of the Map

Men tend to perform better than women at tasks that require spatial skills, such as reading a map, rotating an object in their mind, or finding their way around a new town. Male rats get out of mazes faster than females, and humans follow their example.

> Researchers scanned the brains of men and women as they tried to escape a three-dimensional virtual-reality maze. The volunteers pushed buttons to move their virtual selves left, right or ahead. In the real world, that might be like trying to find a specific place in an unfamiliar city, said neurologist Dr. Matthias Riepe of the University of Ulm in Germany. The men got out of the maze in an average of two minutes and 22 seconds, vs. an average of three minutes and 16 seconds for the women. That fits with previous studies in animals and people that suggest males navigate better in an unfamiliar environment.[8]

In tests where subjects are shown drawings of a complex object from two different views and asked if they are the same object, men consistently score higher than women. The male dominance in this skill begins to show itself even among children. A common test used to determine spatial ability is a water level test where test subjects are shown a drawing of a tilted flask and are asked to indicate the water level. Males tend to show the level as horizontal, which is the correct manner, while females tend to draw the level at the same tilt as the flask. Test results have been dramatic enough to confidently indicate that men are the winners in this contest.

Some people may argue that these differences are based on education or socialization, but a few rare situations give fascinating evidence that these different skill levels have more to do with hormones than external factors. Women who were once exposed to high levels of androgens (hormones that encourage male development) scored more like men on spatial tests.

Let's Talk

Women have a decided advantage in verbal ability. Women are generally better at rapidly coming up with a set of words that belong to a particular category. Language for both men and women is primarily a function of the left hemisphere, but women also tend to have areas of the right hemisphere that produce language. In other words, women use both sides of their brain when communicating.

As a result, men and women are often frustrated with one another in communication. Women are naturally more skilled at it, and they want the men in their lives to rise to their level. Men become aware of their relative inadequacy, compared to their female acquaintances, and they want to avoid the frustration. Men only like to do things they can succeed at, so they are tempted to avoid conversation because the women they know consistently outperform them.

Rosie O'Donnell plays the part of Becky in the movie *Sleepless in Seattle*. She is talking with Meg Ryan, who plays the lead female, Annie Reed. They are talking about the challenge of male-female relationships when Becky concludes, "Verbal ability is a highly overrated thing in a guy, and it's our pathetic need for it that gets us into so much trouble."

The Money Clip

Women often express their love with words, and so they often misunderstand a man's expression of love. Relationship specialist Dr. Phil explains,

> Currency is what matters to people. It's the reward that motivates people to act in a particular way....If you want to influence a man, you need to know what he treasures. Maybe it is money, time, his car....If you want to know how a man feels, pay attention to how he treats what he values. Whatever it is, if he gives you what is precious to him (whether you value it or not), he has performed an act of love that may mean much more to him than any words he might say....I once gave my wife, Robin, a card that pictured a male and a female cat sitting on a fence, looking lovingly at each other and the moon. The male cat says to his girlfriend, "If I had two dead rats, I would give you one![9]

Ladies, take a moment and think of the men in your life—your father, brother, husband. What do each of these men value? What acts of sharing have they done that you may not have seen as acts of love until now? A man may rotate your tires as his way of saying, "I love you." Talk is cheap to a male; actions speak louder than words. What is your husband, your dad, your brother, or your son trying to tell you with his actions?

One day, on my (Pam's) way out the door to a speaking engagement, I said to my sleepy sons, "Love ya. Babe, do me a favor...Dad's going to need some help today, okay?"

Later that day, I discovered that my two sons had carried 30 garage doors, each garage door weighing about 200 pounds, just the two of them, while helping dismantle "Grad Nite." Bill told me they worked eight hours straight without complaint. When I called each of their cell phones to compliment and thank them, they each independent of the other said, "No problem, Mom. Love you." My sons' currency is their time and their physical strength. Love to me that day was expressed by lifting and moving 30 heavy garage doors. How is your man expressing love? If his love were kept in a money clip, what currency would be there: his expertise, his time, his talent, his car? What is he willing to share? Thank him for sharing—he may be sharing his heart. Nothing feels better to a man's heart than a compliment. Appreciation and kindness open a man's heart.

Remember?

A running joke in my (Bill's) relationship with Pam is that she often says, "Remember? I told you." She might have told me, but I often don't remember. As I did some research, I learned I have a pretty normal male brain. Other guys don't always remember either!

Women consistently have better memories than men. The connection of both sides of the brain seems to give women the ability to associate the information of a certain event with its emotional impact, making the memory more vivid and thus more memorable. Positively, women's lives tend to be more vivid, and their ability to recall details is far superior to men's. Experiences are often richer and last longer for them. Negatively, the traumatic events of life live longer also.

Actress Anne Heche reports that she was abused by her father from the time she was a toddler until she was 12 years old. The memory of her abuse was so vivid that it ran her life for years as an adult. She admits, "I did a lot of things in my life to get away from what had happened to me. I drank, I smoked, I did drugs, I had sex....I did anything I could to get the shame out of my life."[10]

The Aggressive Male Brain

Men display aggressive behavior more often and for more reasons than women. A structure in the brain plays an important role in this behavior. It is called the *amygdala*. The structure is about the size of a small nut and is named after the Latin word for *almond*. The amygdala is located beside the hypothalamus and shares numerous connections with it. The nuclei of the amydgala contribute to behaviors that have strong emotional loading—behaviors such as aggression, fear-driven activity, and sexual behavior.

The two nuclei of the amygdala that are related to aggressive behavior are larger in males and are loaded with androgen-sensitive receptors. In research done with male rats, alterations cause a male to avoid females as possible sex partners. In other research, "...lesions of this region in juvenile monkeys reduce rough-and-tumble play behavior."[11] The evidence connects androgens with agressiveness in children and adults.

We certainly do not want to go so far as to say that men cannot choose how aggressive they are, blaming inappropriate behavior on chemistry. Life is more complex than that, and we must factor in training, personal convictions, the restraint of maturity, and social expectations. But at the same time, we would be foolish to ignore the influence of hormones. Pregnant women are well aware of the impact of body chemistry. During the second half of pregnancy, when progesterone levels rise, women show an increase in aggressive behavior. Aggressiveness decreases when the child is born, but it increases again if the baby is allowed to nurse. Breastfeeding stimulates the release of progesterone into the blood system, and this in turn raises aggressive behavior.

Oh, What a Feeling

We all are aware of our emotions, but we have difficulty explaining what they are or how they work. Emotions can be incredibly positive and make our entire body feel good. They can be remarkably negative and make our entire body feel bad. They can be anything in-between and can hit us at any time in reaction to any event in life. Explaining exactly what causes our emotional reactions is difficult, but part of the answer clearly lies in the brain.

Men and women experience emotions at roughly the same pace. They both get happy, sad, frustrated, scared, excited, and so on with regularity. Many people have believed that women are more emotional than men, but in fact, both sexes appear to be equally emotional. This is not to deny the differences, however. Women tend to express their emotions more freely than men and will express those emotions on a wider range. They are more likely to be willing to directly discuss their fears, frustrations, joys, and experiences. As a result, the spouses, kids, and friends of most women know what they are feeling most of the time. Men, on the other hand, look for indirect means to express their emotions. They avoid conversations, give the silent treatment, and get busy. When faced with negative emotions that lead to personal sadness, they look for distractions to get them away from dealing with the issue. They watch television, they work on their cars, they play on their computers, or they work in their yard. What they don't do is readily talk about how they feel.

We have much to learn about how emotions are developed and expressed. Are they learned by experience? Are they the result of processes in the brain? Are they a function of personality? We will search for answers to these questions for years to come.

Fear This

Fear is an emotion that both men and women experience. Men try to act like they are not afraid.

> Question: How many men does it take to change a light-bulb?
> Answer: None. Real men aren't afraid of the dark.

But in reality, life is sometimes dangerous, and fear keeps us alert to the perils. But men and women view fear differently. Women experience fear more often than men. When men think about physical injury, they picture either harm done to their physical body or harm done to some property they own. When women think about physical injury, they assess the emotional impact of someone treating them unfairly or taking advantage of them. Women feel more confident expressing their fear to both men and women.

Researchers have identified two distinct categories of fear. Personal fear relates to fear for ourselves and what might happen to us. Altruistic fear is fear for others and what might happen to them. In the research, women experience more personal fear than men, as might be expected. Contrary to expectations, however, men felt more altruistic fear for members of their family. "Interestingly, 33% of men experienced altruistic fear for their wives, whereas only 10% of the wives experienced altruistic fear for their husbands. In regard to children, however, women experienced more altruistic fear than did men (38% vs. 11%, respectively)."[12]

Fear also accounts for more health problems in men than in women. Men have a tendency to internalize their fear and fight through it. Since fear triggers the fight-or-flight syndrome, adrenaline floods the body, heart rate increases, and blood pressure rises. In the absence of expression and action, these conditions stress the body. Add to this the fact that men are driven to succeed, and the stress builds. A man may experience fear about not being able to keep his commitments, about not being good enough to maintain his relationships, or about being inadequate to provide the way he thinks is best. Eventually, the tough-guy routine that men are so good at takes its toll.

In close relationships, such as marriage, men and women handle their fear differently. Men generally withdraw and withhold their fear, while women are more likely to share their fear. Many people think men are quiet because their feelings aren't as intense. But just the opposite seems true. Researcher John Gottman discovered that men withdraw because they get "flooded" with emotions when they discuss important and sensitive issues in their relationships. They appear to become overwhelmed with the emotional realities of the relationship and run away. Women, on the other hand, are driven to talk about it. They become more confrontational and are willing to use hostile emotional approaches to get the conversation started.[13]

An interesting study recently suggested a physical source of fear. The study involved stimulating a certain portion of the front of the brain in rats while they were in a situation that causes fear. Stimulating this area caused fear to disappear as if a switch were turned off. This area of the brain is connected to other areas that are associated with memories of fear. Stimulating this area seems to create memories of safety. This leads us to believe that the way we process emotions is probably closely associated with the makeup of the brain.[14]

Anger

Anger is another common emotion men and women both experience. Anger prepares your body to fight. Adrenaline and hormones are dumped into your bloodstream, your blood pressure increases, your heart rate rises, and your breathing gets faster. All of this gets your body ready to either run like crazy or fight like a champion. Anger is a normal emotional reaction to the risky experiences of life and can be very healthy. Men and women get angry for a lot of the same reasons. For instance, when they feel they have been mistreated or they are being treated in a condescending way, both men and women feel the mercury rising. Men, however, experience angry responses when they are in physical or chaotic situations—when a fight is imminent, a project won't cooperate, or they are being directly challenged by another person. Women, on the other hand, experience anger when they are faced with uncontrollable situations—the car breaks down, a snowstorm hits, or expectations get out of control.

Although anger can be productive, chronic anger that creates stubborn, rigid, and impatient attitudes is destructive to your relationships and hurts your body. It raises your blood pressure and can make you more susceptible to heart attacks and strokes. You hurt other people's feelings and lose their trust. Rather than hang around you and receive abusive treatment, they keep their distance.

Expressing your anger helps. Men who express their anger rather than holding it in experience fewer heart problems and strokes. Women experience fewer health problems related to anger because they are better at expressing it. Men would do well to learn to be more expressive when they feel angry.

But men are not as good at talking about their anger as women, and they are more aggressive because of high levels of testosterone. Once men decide that holding anger in is a bad idea, they can easily go overboard. Their aggressive nature can supersede their ability to express themselves emotionally. They go from not expressing anger to expressing too much anger. Some men seem to have a built-in tendency to become batterers, while women almost never batter men. These men are unpredictable, unable to respond to their wives, and impossible to prevent from battering once an argument has begun. They have not learned to appropriately express their anger, so they seek to control and intimidate the women in their lives through physical aggression. The battering is almost always accompanied by emotional abuse, often involves injury, and virtually always causes fear in the battered women. Rather than being expressive, these men become explosive. Rather than step up, they blow up.

If this is you, for the sake of your health and the survival of your relationships, you need to learn appropriate ways to express your anger. This may take professional help, and you will need to humbly seek out new skills, but the payoff is huge. Your loved ones like you better, and men who directly express anger are 50 percent less likely to have a stroke than men who express anger by slamming doors or making sarcastic or nasty remarks, according to a Harvard School of Public Health study.[15] Men will be aggressive in their approach to life, but they cannot afford to cross the line into explosive anger.

A Great Idea

Often, an angry discussion leads to growth in a relationship. We actually believe that husbands and wives argue because they love each other. Parents and children argue because they love each other. This is true for two reasons. First, in loving family relationships, everything you do impacts the lives of those you love. The way you spend money, make decisions, clean up after yourself, and organize have a profound and daily influence on everyone in your family.

I (Bill) have a pretty productive family. I enjoy that about them and have a lifetime of memories based on their athletic, academic, and community achievements. I consistently have to come to grips with the fact that productivity and spending money go together. My kids are constantly telling me about something that I need to pay for. They need new cleats, new shoes, new uniforms, new books, spending money, lunch money, money to lose in the hole in their pockets, and so on. I often feel as if I were an ATM, and my kids believe the bank is always full. In fact, my boys have started telling me they need money rather than asking for money. My response now is, "Thanks for sharing that with me." The first time I said that, they looked at me with a shocked look as if I had just insulted their best friend. Then they realized what I meant, and they asked. They even included a "please"!

The second reason anger and arguments are common is that the very thing you love most about people is the thing that drives you crazy. Pam is a very creative individual. That is one of the reasons I was attracted to her. Her creativity has filled our life with memories and has kept our life very interesting. She is constantly brewing ideas for making the world a better place. But for the first ten years of our marriage, this wonderful trait of hers caused a lot of turmoil. We would set aside an evening just for us. I would move into a relaxing waffle-box and assume we would have a nice evening casually sharing our lives. Pam saw these nights as an opportunity to share with me all the things she has been thinking about. When I share ideas with Pam, I have usually thought them through and am ready for us to implement them. I am now seeking her input to make sure I am on the right track. I didn't realize Pam shares her ideas simply because she has them.

Here is how the conversation would go. She would share the first idea, and I would begin thinking, *Okay, this is a big idea, but I trust Pam, and I think we can do this.* About that time, she would share her second big idea. I would ponder, *I want to be a good husband, and even though this could be a challenge, we are pretty energetic people, so I think we can fit both of these ideas in.* Then she would share the third idea, and I would begin to think, *This woman is crazy. There is no way we can do all three of these.* And then the fourth idea comes pouring out. My response at this point was, *If I don't stop her, she is going to ruin our lives!* I would either get angry with her, or I would shut down and leave Pam confused about what just happened. In her mind we were just talking, but in my mind we were ruining our lives.

After ten years (I was a slow learner), I realized she had not attempted to implement most of the ideas she had shared, so I asked her, "Pam, are all these ideas important?"

Her response was, "Of course. They're my ideas."

I said, "Wrong question. What I really mean is, do I have to do something with every idea you share?"

She responded, "Of course not. I don't even act on all my ideas."

"Pam, when you share an idea that I don't want to do anything with, can I just say, 'That's a great idea'?"

Her response was simply, "That's a great idea!"

My anger led to us clarifying one of the things we love about our relationship. In marriage, the woman usually initiates conversations that involve anger. She seems to have a better sense of the emotional balance that maintains health in the relationship, and she has an arsenal of methods for bringing up difficult conversations. For example, she may choose the dreaded, "Honey, we need to talk." Or she may use the backdoor approach. You notice that something is out of balance, but when you ask, "What's wrong, dear?" she answers with, "Nothing," in a way that lowers the temperature in the house by three degrees. Alternatively, she may consider crying. This gets her husband's attention because he interprets tears as weakness, and he feels needed. He will enter the conversation to try to be heroic in some way. Finally, she may resort to *the look*. It is a silent look, but it speaks volumes. It sends shivers up and down the spine of the intended victim. Only women can do it! When men try, they are comical. With women it is tactical. Our theory is that *the look* went with the rib that God took from Adam and used to form Eve. Nobody enjoys the onset of these conversations, but she initiates the negative interaction because it often becomes a positive experience for the relationship as she and her husband discuss difficult but vital issues.

The Art of Acceptance

Since the brains of men and women are connected differently, we must expect different behavior from each. The differences cannot be erased because they relate to our physical makeup. Certainly growth and maturity are required by all of us, but to think that maturity will erase the way connections are made in the brain is ridiculous. Ideas are like children—our own are always the greatest! So give grace, and keep the discovery process going.

> After church on Sunday morning, a young boy suddenly announced to his mother, "Mom, I've decided I'm going to be a minister when I grow up."
>
> "That's great," the mother said, "but what made you decide to be a minister?"
>
> "Well," the boy replied, "I'll have to go to church on Sunday anyway, and I figure it will be more fun to stand up and yell than to sit still and listen."

> One woman was frustrated with her husband and reported this story. After arguing with her husband one day, she left in frustration and went shopping. At the check-out counter, the clerk noticed a remote control for a television set sticking out of her purse.
>
> "Do you always carry your TV remote?" the clerk asked.
>
> "No," the woman replied. "But my husband refused to come shopping with me, so I figured this was the most evil thing I could do to him!"

Why Did You Do That?

1. What did you learn about the male mind that helps you understand your spouse?

2. What did you learn about the female mind that helps you understand your spouse?

3. What did you learn that can enhance your relationship?

4. As you think of the way the male and female minds work, what new insight will help you at home? At work? In social settings?

5. From what you have read thus far, do you think certain roles or jobs are easier for one gender than the other? Explain.

6. Who is someone of the opposite gender you can compliment for the way their mind works? (You might want to go in a circle and allow each person to compliment someone of the opposite gender).

Imagine the Creator as a stand-up comedian—
and at once the world becomes explicable.
—H. L. MENCKEN

Physical Differences

A perfect man met a perfect woman. After a perfect courtship, they had a perfect wedding. Their life together, of course, was perfect. One snowy, stormy Christmas Eve, this perfect couple was driving along a winding road when they noticed someone at the roadside in distress. Being the perfect couple, they stopped to help.

There stood Santa Claus with a huge bundle of toys. Not wanting to disappoint any children on the eve of Christmas, the perfect couple loaded Santa and his toys into their vehicle. Soon they were delivering toys together.

Unfortunately, the driving conditions deteriorated, and the perfect couple and Santa Claus had an accident. Only one of them survived the accident.

Question: Who was the survivor?

Woman's answer: The perfect woman! She's the only one that really existed in the first place. Everyone knows neither Santa Claus nor a perfect man really exist.

Man's response: With no perfect man and no Santa Claus, the perfect woman must have been driving. This explains the accident.

In the Beginning

In the beginning, God created a man. His name was Adam, and he and God had a great relationship. They walked in the garden and shared the adventure of life together. Adam's life had purpose and spiritual vitality in a perfect environment. Adam was a remarkable feat of creation because God made him in His own image.

But Adam was only half the story. The image of God was too glorious and too big to be reflected in a man. And so God created a woman. God had taken a good look at His creation and had concluded that almost everything was good. The sky was magnificent, the foliage was in full bloom, and the animals were vibrantly alive, but mankind was not complete. And so God created Eve. She made a perfect environment even better.

In this great act of creation, God declared that men and women are the pinnacle of His creative efforts and possess equal value. God had plans for a great partnership between Himself and the people He created. He desired to guide them while they subdued the earth and built a great society. But Adam and Eve decided they had a better plan and took things into their own hands. They rebelled against God's plan, and their hearts became corrupted. Men and women have been trying to figure each other out ever since.

You have probably heard some statements that reflect this frustration.

- Question: What is the difference between a man and a savings bond?
  Answer: The savings bond matures!

- For Sale by Owner: complete set of Encyclopedia Britannica. 45 volumes. Excellent condition. No longer needed. Got married last weekend. Wife knows everything.

- To be happy with a man, you must understand him a lot and love him a little. To be happy with a woman, you must love her a lot and not try to understand her at all.

Risky Business

Men seek out risk and danger more often than women. Little boys hit, chase, and create battles with one another on a daily basis. Just this week I watched my 12-year-old son bait his 19-year-old brother into a fight. His older brother is a finely tuned college football player. Muscles bulge in his body. He works out with 300-pound men. But none of this mattered to our 12-year-old. He walked up to this brother, hit him, and waited to be pummeled. As his brother picked him up, he said, "Oh, no! I'm in trouble now!" But he was laughing the whole time!

Women often wonder why men are attracted to risky behavior, risky investments, and risky activities. As men, we love to hike, hunt, and look for the edge in whatever we are pursuing. Risk is built into a man's makeup. We are more likely to get sick, likely to die younger, more likely to have some physical struggle. From the womb, we develop in a more risky physical state. We are physically strong and consider risk a challenge. For women, this is a learned skill. Physically, they are more stable and safe. They develop with fewer problems. They get used to things going well early on. So, throughout life the girls are wondering why the boys are taking so many chances, and the boys are wondering why the girls don't want to have any fun.

Body Language

In every culture where the issue has been studied, men are about 7 percent taller than women. The average untrained man is about 30 percent stronger than a woman his own age. Men can generally run faster than women, and they can continue strenuous physical activity for a longer period of time. Women also have smaller shoulders, larger hips, carry more fat, and have a smaller limb-to-body length ratio.[1]

Men have a decided advantage in weight lifting and sheer athletic performance. Their muscles break down lactic acid more efficiently than do women's, so they avoid cramping easier. Women have been working out more and developing their athletic ability, but they will probably never equal men in such athletic competitions as sprinting, wrestling, and weight lifting.

Young boys and adult men are very aware of their physical strength. Every year I lead a father-son camping trip that has a dramatic impact on all the men who attend. Some years we head to the mountains and fish in lakes and streams. Some years we travel to Mexico and fish in the Gulf of California. Some years we go to Catalina Island, where we fish in the ocean and snorkel along the coast. The common theme of these trips is physical exertion to overcome a strenuous goal. To some, the trip looks like a recreational outing designed to help us escape reality. But the trips are designed to touch a chord that lies deep in the soul of our sons. Men learn when they are pushed to their limits. When a young man has overcome a physical challenge, his confidence in every area of life grows. When he overcomes a fearful situation, his focus in all areas of life becomes clearer.

We were camping on the Colorado River with three Jet Skis. One of the young men with us was not endowed with great athletic ability, but he still had a man-sized drive to face challenges. So when his time came to ride, he jumped on and took off. After about 30 minutes, his partner came back to camp and told us that this young man had fallen off his Jet Ski and couldn't get back on. He was now drifting downstream, holding onto his vehicle. I grabbed Caleb, who was 11 years old at the time, and jumped on our watercraft to rescue him. When I reached the young man, he was holding on to his Jet Ski, helplessly floating down the Colorado River.

I told my son that he would have to drive the vehicle we were riding so I could help. I turned the controls over to him and jumped in the water. I attempted to stabilize the Jet Ski so this 16-year-old could struggle back up. We worked at it for about 15 minutes. Every attempt failed. The whole time, Caleb was riding the other Jet Ski with remarkable skill. I felt contrasting emotions while I was in the water. I felt sorry for this young man because his ego was taking a beating. In his heart he wanted to successfully climb to the seat, grab the accelerator, and harness the horsepower of this machine. Instead, he was failing at every level. At the same time, I was incredibly proud of my 11-year-old son because he was doing what his adolescent counterpart could not.

We finally decided that this teenager was not going to get back on his Jet Ski. We needed to get back, so I told him to hold onto the back of the seat while I towed him back to camp. He grabbed on, and we started the long trek back. We had to go slow because he would be surrounded by water if I went too fast. Because of the slow pace, exhaust fumes swirled around his head during the 50-minute trip. As we pulled up to camp, he had to humbly face the other guys, who all saw him get towed into shore. Since guys are relentlessly competitive, they immediately began making fun of him. At the same time, they asked if he was okay.

For the next three hours, he found a quiet spot away from the rest of us. This was an unplanned defining moment of his life. If he didn't face the challenge again, he would shrink with the thought that he was inadequate and not able to keep up with other men. If he faced the challenge and failed again, he would ruin his trip and find a place deep within himself to hide from future challenges. If, however, he overcame the obstacles, he would recover his confidence and resurrect the need to risk that lives in every man. He didn't want to talk about it. He didn't want to analyze it. He wanted—and needed—to overcome it!

Without a word, he finally walked over to the two Jet Skis that were parked on the shore. He walked around them, checking them out as if he were an inspector, analyzing their integrity. We all watched him without interrupting the process. We knew that he was in a moment of passage in manhood. He was asking if he had the courage to take a new risk. He was settling the issue of what kind of a man he really was. These moments engage the sense of risk that beats in our hearts and assaults our bodies.

In a decisive move, he turned the Jet Ski around so the nose was pointing to the middle of the river. He experimented with a couple of different ways of mounting the machine, and then he jumped on. He fired up the engine and took off. Those of us on the shore cheered as he sped off to his new adventure. Shortly, he fell off the ski in the middle of a turn, and we all held our breath. We were disappointed when he grabbed the vehicle and started swimming to shore rather than mounting up again. But, to our surprise, he stopped about 20 yards short of the shore, stood up in the shallower water, and jumped back on.

He had faced the challenge and overcome! The smile on his face was inextinguishable. When he got back to shore, he stood taller and walked straighter. For the next three days, he was more energetic, more talkative, and more cooperative. He had taken a huge step of growth. His ability to overcome the challenge in the water impacted his confidence in every other area of his life. This was a perfect example of a man's need to succeed at the risks in his life.

Survivor

Women, however, have a decided advantage regarding the sheer ability to survive. The very characteristics that put women at a disadvantage in strength activities work in their favor when the going gets really tough. If food is scarce, the larger stores of fat in a woman's body will sustain her longer than a man. Her smaller frame ensures that she loses less heat than a man would in cold climates. Women burn up food and oxygen more slowly, so they require less to keep going and can thus survive for longer periods of time.

Building on the survivor theme in a young woman's life may be wise. Often girls are not encouraged to push themselves physically. Instead, many families coddle and cater to their daughters. This may do them a great disservice. Allowing a young woman to develop the survivor in her will help her later in life when the stakes are much higher.

Immunity

Men pride themselves in being strong and virile, but in reality they are actually much more vulnerable to disease than are women. Consider the following statistics.

- Between 107 and 124 males are conceived for every 100 females. But the male embryo is more likely to abort spontaneously, perhaps by a factor of 135 to 100. As a result, only 106 boys are actually born for every 100 girls.[2]

- Most males survive the birth process, but after birth, a newborn boy is more likely than a girl to die before he is one year old. He is more susceptible to infection and has a greater chance of being born with some congenital illness. Boys are more likely to suffer from the kinds of brain disorders that lead to epilepsy, cerebral palsy, or febrile convulsions.

- In our society, those who live through the first year have an excellent chance of reaching the age of 35. But the majority of those who fail to live that long are men.

- During these years, men are more likely to die in accidents— particularly on the road—and they continue to be more susceptible to fatal infectious diseases.

- Men are more prone to heart attacks and ulcers than are women.

- Despite the fact that more young women try to commit suicide, more young men succeed in doing so.

- As a result, by the age of 35 there are roughly the same number of men and women left alive.[3]

After 40 years of age, the fatal diseases begin to take a heavy toll. Women are more likely than men to suffer from cancer of the reproductive organs and from diseases related to hormones, such as diabetes and thyroid disorders, but men are far more susceptible to most of the other forms of serious illness.

> They are four times more likely to get lung cancer, three times more likely to contract heart disease, and they are also significantly more prone to suffer strokes and disorders of the respiratory system like bronchitis and emphysema. In consequence, the numerical balance between the sexes, which was originally weighted so heavily in favor of the male, now tips the other way, and by the time we get to seventy, there are two women for every man still surviving.[4]

Among those who live to be 100 years old or more, women outnumber men four to one.

Women may worry about more issues in life, but men consistently have higher blood pressure. This may be caused by hormones because the picture changes when women experience menopause. Prior to "the change," men live with higher blood pressure, a greater risk for cardiovascular disease, and an increased susceptibility to problems with their kidneys. In fact, about 30 percent of the incidence of kidney disease is caused by hypertension. After menopause, however, women's blood pressure levels are higher than men's.

The reason for the superior ability of women to maintain their health is related to the fact that they have two X chromosomes. The Y chromosome carries very little genetic code. Its main function is to determine the fact that the individual is male. Sex-related characteristics are primarily carried in the X chromosome. Since men have only one X chromosome, if a gene has a problem, the man will carry that problem his entire life. Women, on the other hand, have a second X chromosome. If they have a problem with a gene, a second corresponding gene carries similar information that can overcome the defective material.

Therefore, X-linked diseases are more common in men than in women. These diseases include color-blindness, hemophilia, rickets, diabetes, immunoglobin deficiency, and hyperthyroidism. For example, color blindness "affects more than one man in twelve but less than one woman in a hundred."[5] The X chromosome appears to be responsible for regulating antibodies that fight off infection. In this day of hearty antibiotics, few deaths are caused by infections. But deaths usually occur during the first year of life, and boys are much more likely to die than girls. Some scientists are suggesting that the extra X chromosome acts as a backup system that gives girls a greater chance of survival.

All in all, being a man is simply more dangerous than being a woman, and the more "male" a person is, the more risks he takes. Men who are given extra male hormones are more likely to die from an early heart attack, and men with less male hormones live longer. A rather strange piece of research comes from the days when patients in mental hospitals were treated with much less dignity than today. "Examination of the medical records of one such hospital in America shows that male patients who had been castrated tended to live an average of thirteen years longer than those who had not."[6]

This is one of the reasons men go through a midlife evaluation. Because of our strength, we tend to think we are invincible. We have survived enough dangerous situations that we mistakenly think we can survive them all. We have lifted heavy objects, done physical chores, run with speed, built things with skill, and so on. When we are suddenly faced with health challenges, we tend to go into shock.

A good friend of ours had a heart attack when he was 40 years old. He was driving home from work one day, when suddenly he felt a sharp pain in his chest that radiated down his left arm. He said to himself, *I think I am having a heart attack—this might be my last chance to have a meatball sandwich.* He knew that the local sandwich shop was having a "two for the price of one" special on meatball sandwiches, so he stopped for one on the way home to get his wife. He ate the other one on the way to the hospital. When he saw the doctor, he was diagnosed with a heart disease and has had to seriously alter his diet.

My friend's experience affected our entire circle of friends. He was in good shape and generally took good care of himself. However, he has a rare condition that will not eliminate any fat from his blood system. Once it gets in, it stays. Every man in our circle instantly became concerned about his health. We couldn't believe our friend was mortal, and we began to wonder, *Could this have happened to me?* Visits to the doctor increased for the whole group. Memberships to health clubs became popular. Some of the men even looked into working with the teenagers in our church in an attempt to recover their youth. Most young men live in denial, but eventually we must face the fact that men suffer more health problems than women.

Although men are wired to take risks and tend to have more health problems, their behavior does not seem to be affected. Men are more likely to be overweight than women. Men are less likely than women to be physically active during their leisure time. Three times as many men as women engage in binge drinking, seven times as many men are chronic drinkers, and three times as many men drive while under the influence of alcohol.[7] With the challenges to health that are built into the male anatomy, we should actually take better care of ourselves. But our need to conquer overwhelms our common sense, and we overdo just about every area of life.

Making Whoopee

Sex is a fascinating and mysterious behavior. Men and women are the only species on earth who engage in sex for the pleasure of the experience. All other species reproduce through sexual activity by instinct. People, on the other hand, are creative in their sexual expression to one another and find it relieves stress, communicates love, and provides recreation in addition to its reproductive function. Our fascination with sexual behavior causes us to think about it, dream about it, hurt over it, hope for it, and laugh about it.

The main difference in the sexual experience of men and women is that climax for men is followed by a very sharp decline in arousal. The penis begins to lose its erection quickly, a pleasant exhaustion sets in and further sexual activity is impossible for a period of time. For women, sexual arousal is maintained for a period of time. Multiple orgasms are possible for the vast majority of women. The fact that many women do not experience a multiple string of orgasms is, in most cases, due to psychological and emotional issues, not physical ability.

Check the Signals

The physical operation of our bodies is vital to keep in mind as we move forward in our lives. Sean moved his family to a new city. His wife, Rachel, was struggling with the new culture. She felt as if she didn't have any friends, although she had always thought of herself as friendly. In addition, Sean, her normally attentive spouse, seemed in a funk. He had been a hardworking, assertive, motivated, and successful businessman. Suddenly, he was lethargic and almost apathetic. Rachel was picking up more and more of his business, trying to help keep it afloat. She felt Sean was disengaged and disinterested in her, the business, and life in general. Rachel was concerned and was asking a lot of questions. *Was his apathy toward her the symptoms of an affair? Was it a midlife crisis? Or was it something worse?* Rachel became more dramatic in her attempts to get Sean's attention. Sean felt his wife was illogical and unreasonable. His wife's drama quickly turned to depression and then self-destructive behaviors.

When they requested counseling, they were encouraged to get physicals. Rachel's doctor discovered her severe mood swings were linked to PMS, and she encouraged Rachel to seek further treatment. Sean's doctor discovered an immune disease. What looked like laziness to Rachel was in reality a quite serious disease. Their marriage improved dramatically when they realized the physical causes of the symptoms they struggled with. No amount of counseling would have determined those causes. A little bit of medicine and large doses of forgiveness and understanding was the prescription for helping this couple get back on track. How about you? What information or enlightenment from this chapter might give you a new view of the opposite gender? Information is the key to unlocking understanding and appreciation.

A woman accompanied her husband to the doctor's office. After his checkup, the doctor called the wife into his office alone. He said, "Your husband is suffering from a very severe disease, combined with horrible stress. If you don't follow my instructions, your husband will surely die. Each morning, fix him a healthy breakfast. Be pleasant, and make sure he is in a good mood. For lunch, make him a nutritious meal. For dinner, prepare an especially nice meal for him. Don't burden him with chores, as he probably had a hard day. Don't discuss your problems with him, or you will make his stress worse. And most importantly, make love with your husband several times a week and satisfy his every whim. If you can do this for the next ten months to a year, I think your husband will regain his health completely."

On the way home, the husband asked his wife, "What did the doctor say?"

"You're going to die," was her reply.

If Men Had Babies...

- Maternity leave would last two years—with full pay.
- Researchers would find a cure for stretch marks.
- Natural childbirth would become obsolete.
- Morning sickness would rank as the nation's number one health problem.

- All methods of birth control would be 100 percent effective.
- Children would be kept in the hospital until toilet trained.
- Men would be eager to talk about commitment.
- Men wouldn't think twins were so cute.
- Sons would have to be home from dates by 10:00 P.M.
- Briefcases would double as diaper bags.
- Paternity suits would be a fashion line of clothes.
- Men would stay in bed during the entire pregnancy.
- Restaurants would include ice cream and pickles as main entrees.
- Women would rule the world.

Why Did You Do That?

1. From what you read, is one sex weaker than the other? Which one?

2. The genders are equal but different. Do you agree or disagree?

3. What health concerns should you be watchful of for your husband? For your wife?

4. What are the advantages of being male? Of being female?

5. What are the disadvantages of being male? Of being female?

6. Did you gain any information or were you reminded of any information that can lead to greater understanding of the opposite gender?

7. What did you gain from this chapter that gives you more appreciation or respect for the opposite gender?

Better keep yourself clean and bright;
you are the window through which you must see the world.
—George Bernard Shaw

The Influence of Family

Zachery, our middle son, is a very creative person. He expresses his creativity in almost everything he does, and signs of his originality fill our home—even our kitchen cupboards.

When Zachery was eight, I showed him how to put away the dishes after dinner. I demonstrated stacking everything neatly and putting larger items on the bottom, smaller items on top. But one day, I opened the cupboard and witnessed the most precarious collection of dishes I had ever seen. Glasses teetered in every conceivable direction. Plates leaned at all angles.

In frustration I yelled out, "Zachery, get in here!"

He came running in with a very proud look on his face despite my raised voice.

"Zachery, what is this?" I barked as I pointed at the strange collection of dishes.

He looked up at me with big eyes, and with utter confidence he said, "A volcano, Dad. Can't you see it?"

I was dumbfounded. All I could say was, "You're right, Zachery. It's a volcano." Then I silently closed the cupboard and walked away.

The Story of Your Life

The story of your life has never been told before. Your story has some elements that are common to everyone else, but the elements have never, and will never, come together in exactly the same way as they come together in your life. Your story is made up of your sex, your personality, your life experiences, your emotions, your passions, and your setbacks. These are the ingredients that make up your unique story, and they are all poured into your life and mixed together in the context of your family.

In this chapter, we will show how the families we grew up in shaped the story of our lives. We hope that our stories will help you understand more about the story of your life as you continue to discover why you act the way you do. Your family is the place where you worked out who you are. Being either male or female got the ball rolling in your life. Your sex gave you the raw material you have to work with, but your family helped you shape your resources. How has your family influenced the story of your life?

A Place of Love

Ideally, the members of your family are the people who love you the most. They gave birth to you, changed your diapers, cleaned up your messes, and put up with you during the terrible twos. They witnessed the best moments of your life, and they saw you at your worst. They interacted with you during the most important developmental stages of your life. As a result, your relationship with your family has given definition to your understanding of love. Your experience at home helped determine your understanding of a loving relationship. If your family was affectionate, then affection and love are linked in your heart. If your family was encouraging, then encouragement and love go hand in hand for you. If you grew up with anger, then for you, anger and love go together.

I (Bill) grew up in a home that was a strange combination of affection, high moral values, creativity, and paranoia. My parents love me as much as any parents ever have loved their children. When I was young, they showered me with hugs and words of affirmation. I knew my parents were proud of me, and I knew they cared deeply about my life. I also knew that I was expected to do what was right. My dad had an incredibly high sense of integrity. He did what was right because it was right. He avoided what was wrong because it was wrong. Choices were just that simple to my dad. As a result, I learned early in life that if you love someone, you do what is right for him or her. You treat people with respect, and you commit to high morals in all you do. As a result, my heart is softer toward people when I do what is right.

My mom was a very creative individual. She painted, sewed, decorated, and lived with great creativity. We lived in Southern California, and she loved to be in the studio audience at game shows. When I was young, *Let's Make a Deal* was very popular. To get on the show, people had to dress up in a costume and audition while they stood in line. Only the most creative, energetic, and outgoing people would make the show. My mom got on every time. For me, creativity is a normal part of life, and being around creative people is like being with family.

But mixed in with the affection, high morals, and creativity was fear. My mom was afraid of bugs, afraid of modern life, and afraid of people. She had a strange sense that people were out to get her and her family. She often thought people were following her. She dealt with her fear through control. She frantically attempted to control everything in her life. She systematically isolated her kids from anything but school so that she could keep tabs on us. She gradually eliminated all her friendships so no one could intrude in her life. She convinced my dad to buy a cabin in the mountains so we didn't have to interact with the neighbors on weekends. We had some great times in the mountains, but we also had some very stressful weekends because we were running away from...from what?

I feel very comfortable around people who struggle in life. I meet with people weekly who are in crisis in relationships or who are stuck in some personal struggle in life. I have never been intimidated by these situations because I grew up around them. In fact, I feel very much at home helping people move beyond their fear to discover the real potential of their lives.

I (Pam) was raised in a teeny tiny town in Oregon. I was the oldest child, and from my earliest memories of grade school, I remember thinking I had to be perfect to be accepted and feel loved. I wanted an A-plus on all my papers, I wanted to be the best in my dance class, and anything less meant I felt like a failure. Once, when I was eight years old, I took a ballet class with girls much older than myself—mostly high school students. My teacher corrected my posture, and I ran to the bathroom and locked myself in. My mom and the teacher spent nearly an hour talking me out. I seemed to always be in tears because I felt like a failure—even though I was an obedient little girl and an "A" student. Why would someone so young be so hard on herself?

My biological father loved me deeply, often making great sacrifices for me, especially financially—but my dad had a pain deep in his heart, and he chose to answer that pain with alcohol rather than a relationship with God. Living with my dad was a "Jekyll and Hyde" experience. Dad would lovingly waltz me around the living room—and a short time later he would lash out in anger. Whenever he drank, he changed.

The roots of perfectionism were planted in my life at home. My seventh-grade report card showed my grades at 100 percent in six classes and 99.9 percent in one class. My dad had been drinking when he saw my report card, and he said, "Pam, why isn't that last one a 100?" I remember wondering if I would ever be good enough to earn his love.

At the same time, I had a wonderful, creative, goal-setting, nurturing mother. I believe she absorbed much of the trauma of our home. She stood between me and the wrath of my father. Because Dad traveled, our home was happy and safe for five days a week and a potential hurricane for two. Mom invested in our lives during the week while she built up the strength to stand up to my father on the weekend.

As a result, I learned that deep commitment, high expectations, and unexpected reactions were part of a loving relationship. I discovered early that relationships are a little bit chaotic and that deep devotion is necessary to make them work. At the same time, I learned that loving families find ways to be creative, set goals, and make the best of every situation. And when I travel, which I often do, I remember that my dad's job never prohibited us from learning to love each other deeply.

A Place of Values

Your family communicates certain values through every conversation and every activity. Deliberately or accidentally, families pass these values from one generation to another.

My (Bill's) dad loved his work. He was an aeronautical engineer who helped get the Apollo mission to the moon and helped design the engines for the space shuttle. He survived the layoffs of the 60s and worked for the same company for more than 30 years. He regularly said, "I can't believe they pay me to do this job. I would do it for free if I could afford to." My dad's example cemented a legacy in the hearts of my sister, my brother, and myself. We all believe that we should find work that we love to do. This is one of the ways we choose our careers. Dad never verbalized this value, but his example spoke louder than words.

Balance was another big thing for my parents. Work was a high priority for my dad, but so was a peaceful existence. My dad was not fond of stress. He turned down promotions at work because he knew they would increase the stress in his life. He worked hard to balance time for work with time for the family and time for personal hobbies. He also planned financially and balanced the demands of today with the needs of retirement. He was visibly stressed only when things were out of balance.

However, because of my mom's need to control our environment, we valued independence. We didn't get involved in church because we couldn't control the reactions of that many people. We didn't get involved in community activities for the same reason. My mom's example subtly but firmly taught us that we were self-sufficient. We honestly believed that we didn't need other people to have a complete life. Only when I became an adult did I realize what a small life I had lived. It was controlled, predictable, and small. I had missed out on the richness of a diversity of friendships. I had been excluded from the synergy of a group of gifted individuals that banded together for a unified cause. I had not experienced the fullness that comes when my weaknesses are filled in by someone else's strength and vice versa. I had to make a conscious choice to value interdependence over independence.

My (Pam's) family has always been about hard work and loyalty. My grandparents ran a farm their entire lives. They raised sheep, chickens, dairy cattle, alfalfa, and hay. They worked from sunup to sundown for decades. When the chicken shed caught fire, Grandma ran across the field and into the coop to rescue the poultry. For most of their adult life, everything revolved around the milking schedule. At their sixtieth wedding anniversary, I asked Grandma what the secret of their success was. Grandma looked at Grandpa, then looked at me and said with a sly grin, "Pure grit and determination." My mom was raised on the farm and picked up her parents' work ethic. My dad, an itinerant pea harvester when he was 14, worked his way up to the service manager position for Massey Ferguson tractors. My uncles, aunts, cousins—everyone in my family knows how to work hard. So of course, I value hard work.

My family is also remarkably loyal. They have had a lot of personal problems, including divorce, lost jobs, and serious illnesses. Through it all, they have stayed connected to one another and cared for one another. Family reunions are a major priority, and family members travel from all over the country to attend. My dad's oldest sister even bought a piece of property in Colorado and committed to build a family cabin just to create another reason to get together.

Bill and I visited my dad shortly after we were married. My dad and I entered into a very spirited conversation about politics, morals, and religion. We raised our voices and were very passionate about our views. The loyalty in our family enabled us to talk about anything. Our opinions never threatened our relationship because our bond was unbreakable.

But Bill didn't grow up with this kind of interaction. He asked me later that evening, "Pam, why do you and your dad fight all the time?"

"We weren't fighting," I answered.

"You two were yelling at each other!" Bill said.

"We weren't yelling at each other."

"Yes, you were. Your voices kept getting louder, and you looked like you were mad at each other," Bill argued with me.

"Bill, you just don't understand. This is how my family is. We argue with each other, but we are deeply committed to one another, so it doesn't matter."

Loyalty is therefore one of the things I value most in life. I am deeply committed to the people in my life, and I believe that friends can work through anything.

A Place of Definition

Your family has a culture that defines who you are. The roles that families expect men and women to conform to are part of this culture. Families demonstrate their way to handle stress. They set expectations about how much money you should earn and who your social circles should include. They shape the way you dress, the things that bring you joy, and the traditions you celebrate throughout the year.

My (Pam's) family includes generations of cowboys. My mother's grandpa is a native of New Zealand, where his family raised sheep for generations. All of his sons learned how to ride a horse by age three. My dad's family is from Oklahoma, where his family has ridden horses and roped cattle since the turn of the twentieth century. They wear cowboy pants, don cowboy hats, and drive pickup trucks. When life is demanding they "cowboy up." When they face a setback in life, they "cowboy up." That means they suck in their emotions and do what needs to be done—with no complaints. They never give up.

Because of their roots, people in my family have a very traditional view of gender roles. Men work outside the home in physically demanding careers. They fix the cars, fix the fences, and mow the grass. They eat the food the women cook and look for ways to defend them from danger. The women focus on domestic chores. They cook, clean, sew, manage the house, and share their skills with the other women in the community. Kids learn to treat adults with respect. They are seen and not heard when the adults gather.

My dad agreed with a lot of these roles, but he wanted to provide his kids with opportunities that were larger than the context of his immediate family. He wanted each of us to finish college and discover our abilities, and he knew we would never be able to if we were locked too tightly in these traditional roles. He moved away from his family and committed to giving us kids the opportunity to participate in sports, to be involved with 4-H, and to join dance clubs. He believed these experiences, coupled together with a traditional understanding of family, would give us a head start in life.

My dad's plan worked for us. I strongly believe that parents should be the main caregivers for their children, especially during the children's preschool years. Families are the foundation of society and should be carefully protected. People should have the opportunity to develop their potential and diligently apply themselves to the pursuit. I chose to be home with my kids before they started school so I could instill in them the skills and confidence they needed to succeed. But I also continued to grow as an individual so that when they entered school I could begin my career and make my own mark on my generation.

My (Bill's) family was a little different. My dad's father passed away when Dad was 17 years old. My dad didn't talk about his dad much, so I didn't have much history about what a man was supposed to be. My mom's family had a lot of turmoil in it—infighting, competition, and alcohol abuse. Early in their marriage, my mom and dad had conflicts with their families and broke communication with them. In addition, my mom used a lot of reverse psychology to motivate us while she protected herself. So I heard a mixed message throughout my childhood. Sometimes I heard, "You don't have what it takes. You will never be anything in life." At other times she would say, "I am so proud of you." My mom was the strongest personality in my home, so I entered my adult years a little confused. I wasn't sure if I was supposed to be confident or self-conscious.

My mom's need to control her life disallowed struggles in my home. Problems in my life put pressure on my mom to find solutions or to get involved with others to solve the struggles. I learned pretty early that struggles were not acceptable, and asking for help was a sign of weakness. I was a bed wetter until I completed the sixth grade. (This is a much more common condition than most of us are aware of because it is embarrassing to talk about.) When I was in the fifth grade, my mom got tired of dealing with the problem so I slept in a bath-tub on an air mattress for the next two years of my life. At the time, I didn't think anything about this arrangement because it was what I knew. As I now look back on the experience, I realize it added to the process of my shutting down. I had watched my sister and brother try to overcome my mom's influence, and I concluded I couldn't. My defense mechanism was to shut down certain parts of my personality so that I wouldn't be hurt.

As a result, by the time I was 17, I had lost the ability to stand up for myself and make strategic decisions. Just before my senior year in high school, my parents and I went on vacation. I was the youngest of three children. (My sister had moved to Boston, and my brother had left home because of a big conflict with my mom in which my mom falsely accused him of being secretly married.) My dad stayed with us for the first week of vacation and then went home during the second week to work. My mom and I stayed for the second week.

During that week, my mom enrolled me in a brand-new high school without talking with my dad. I figured my dad would return the next weekend and straighten everything out, but much to my dismay, he agreed to let my mom and me live in a new community while he lived three hours away and visited on weekends. I left a familiar school where I was a varsity basketball team starter and had a supportive group of friends. I moved to a brand-new school where I lived in a travel trailer. To this day, I still don't know why I went along with it. Most teenage boys would have said no and driven themselves back home to live with Dad. But not me. I passively went along with the plan and made the best of a bad situation.

A Place of Personal Character

The character qualities you consider important in life were developed in the context of your family. Positive qualities like honesty, integrity, trustworthiness, hard work, perseverance, and follow-through are learned through family interaction. Likewise, negative traits such as manipulation, deception, guilt and shame, underachieving, and laziness are also set in place.

Most families teach a combination of these positive and negative traits at the same time. In my (Bill's) family, telling the truth was expected and modeled. My dad, who had a high sense of moral character, consistently told the truth and trained us kids to do the same. At times he was very patient in the process; sometimes he was not.

When I was five years old, we lived in Sacramento, California, adjacent to an open field. My parents hired a babysitter one day and went out for an extended date. The babysitter locked us out of the house during the afternoon, so I went through the neighborhood looking for something to do. I hooked up with a friend, and we explored together. After about an hour we found a book of matches. The first thing we found to light was a dead fish head, but it didn't burn. We walked to the field next to my house and wondered if we could light a little bit of grass and stomp it out. The little bit of grass lit, and we quickly snuffed it out. We started feeling powerful, so we tried again.

But this time we let the grass burn a little longer before we stomped it out. Before long, the fire picked up momentum and spread across the field.

We ran to the house and frantically knocked on the door. The babysitter angrily answered the door and then panicked when we told her the field was on fire. She called the fire department and then ran to the back yard, grabbed the hose, and started spraying the back fence. The first fire truck extinguished the fire but also got stuck in the field. Another truck had to tow the first one out. Fortunately, none of the houses caught fire even though half the field was blackened. My parents came home after the drama was over, and then we talked.

"Bill, did you start the fire in the field?" my parents asked, already knowing the answer.

Instead of answering the question, I asked one of my own. "Will I get in trouble if I say that I did?" What a silly question! Of course I would be punished. My parents wouldn't be responsible if they didn't punish me. But still they were patient.

"You will get in a lot less trouble if you tell the truth than if you lie to us," they said with kindness in their eyes. They were honest and expected me to be honest. I would always get in more trouble for lying than I would for owning up to my responsibility. By the time I taught this trait to my kids, it was already deeply ingrained in my thinking.

My (Pam's) family taught me that initiative is vital to success. My mom dragged me to retirement homes to perform for the shut-ins. We all raised sheep for the county fair. We all took turns cleaning manure in the barns so that we would learn to not be too proud. We were the family who set up for community events and helped put everything away when they were over. We were involved in most of the compassionate projects in our community, and my mom saw that we took the lead in reaching out to those who were less fortunate than us. I noticed early on that we were doing more than the average family, and this seemed unfair. When I complained to my mom, she simply said, "We are not like other families." I didn't like her answer at the time, but I have come to value that statement like gold. "We are not like other families" has become a motto that reminds me that taking initiative means doing what others are not willing to do. The goals in life that mean the most to me require me to do what others are not willing to do.

A Place of Familiarity

Every family tree has its trends. Family trees commonly have lines of successful professionals, or generation after generation of ministers or manufacturers or entrepreneurs. They also commonly include a chain of alcoholism or divorce or abuse. The generations previous to yours have created a legacy and passed it on from generation to generation. Most people don't deliberately choose to be comfortable with the trends. They just accept them without thinking.

In both of our families, alcohol has had a huge impact. I (Pam) often say alcohol is the sap that runs through the family tree. Not everyone on the tree has a problem with it, but every branch has felt its influence.

As I (Pam) mentioned earlier, my own father was an alcoholic with a severe anger problem. He regularly became verbally violent to every member of my family as he lashed out hurtful, stinging words. My father was also consistently suicidal. I feared for my life every time I was in the car with my dad. He started drinking at breakfast and drank all day. He was a functioning alcoholic. Brilliant at his job, he could perform better drunk than most people could sober, so people excused his behavior. As a child, when I approached Dad, I never knew if he was going to be lovey-dovey or give me the backside of his hand—or worse, his cruel, critical remarks.

When I came home from a date, I begged God to not let my dad be passed out on the front lawn in his underwear. Even worse, Dad was sometimes still awake. Then, in a drunken, slurring stupor, he sat and talked with my date, usually with another beer in his hand.

One day, I drove home from college. My dad had been drinking, so of course he was arguing with Mom. I looked at my brother and sister and said, "I don't know about you guys, but I'm tired of this. Do you want to go for a drive?" The answer was yes, and we left. Not knowing where to go, we just drove and parked in a cornfield.

I said, "I don't remember a lot of stuff from church, but we should probably pray for Mom and Dad." So we did, and then we drove back home. As we entered the house, we could hear Dad yelling. That was normal at our house, and at about midnight we went to bed.

About three A.M. we heard my mom screaming for help. The three of us bolted from our beds into the dark, looking for Mom. I remember thinking, "Oh no, Dad's anger has escalated. We have to rescue Mom!" We raced from room to room to room but we couldn't find Mom. We could just hear her screaming for help!

Finally, my brother, who was a football player, burst into the garage and found my dad trying to hang himself from the rafters. Mom was screaming for anyone who could help Dad. My brother pulled Dad down, dragged him into the house, and pushed him on to the sofa. I knelt on my dad's chest. All four of us could barely hold Dad down while he kept yelling that he wanted to die. Amid the emotional confusion, I looked at my siblings and Mom and said, "I think Dad needs us to pray." So we prayed for Dad, and he calmed a bit. He was still thrashing a little when I remembered the story from Sunday school about David, who played for the king when he acted crazy like this. "We should sing!" I proclaimed. So we sang every song we could think of that came from church.

Dad calmed more but was still upset. I remembered that Dad liked the song "Amazing Grace" because he'd heard it as a kid. So we sang "Amazing Grace" over and over and over again. Dad finally passed out as the sun rose.

I pulled a blanket up over Dad and then looked at my mom and my sister and my brother. We were all exhausted. They headed to bed, but I went to diving practice, hoping to find peace and solace in the water. I didn't tell anyone what had happened at my house.

I (Bill) didn't know much about my family until my grandmother's funeral. We had not seen the family for years, and no one had been willing to talk about the obvious tension in the family. Grandma's pass-ing seemed to give people permission to talk. I found out that both my grandparents on my mom's side were alcoholics and had often been violent with each other. They had both brought people home from bars, bringing turmoil into the lives of their three daughters. When my grandma drank, she became illogical and chaotic and even trashed my parents' house one day while we were away.

For both of our families, alcohol is far too familiar. A majority of the men in the family trees have found alcohol to be a close, though deceptive, friend. As a result, future generations must take a strong stand on abstaining from alcohol use. For any of us, the first drink may be the entrance to a long, hard roller-coaster ride.

A Place of Destiny

God is at work in every family on earth. He knows the victories and the failures of everyone you are related to. He knows that every person in every family needs to be redeemed from the fallen state of human nature. When God sent His only Son to earth to die as the Savior of the world, He was thinking of every family that would ever walk through the halls of history. Therefore, every family has a story of redemption. Somehow, through the legacy of your family, God is bringing salvation to a desperate world. As you explore the history of your family, you will discover a thread of God's redemptive work all along the way. It is obvious in some families and hard to see in others, but it is there.

I (Bill) have discovered a couple of ministers in my dad's back-ground, although I know very little about them. In addition, my mom grew up in Georgia, where owning a Bible and living a life of honor are important values. As a result, my mom bought me a Bible when I was very young because every Southern family bought their chil-dren Bibles. My dad had no passion for any kind of religious life, and we attended church very infrequently, but he was not opposed to my mom's purchase. That Bible ended up being a very strategic addition to my life.

In high school I dealt with the craziness of my family by getting very involved in sports. I played football and basketball and worked hard to become the best athlete I could. I lifted weights regularly and kept myself in good shape throughout the year. I even feigned the athlete's swagger. I tried to convince myself I could handle anything because I was strong and skilled and getting stronger every day.

One day, my best friend asked me if I wanted to spend the night with him and go see the movie *The Exorcist.* Fear danced through my heart, but I convinced myself I could handle the content. I had heard that the demon possession portrayed in the movie was based on some true stories, though I was sure Hollywood had exaggerated the effects. As I watched the movie, I saw a spiritual world I had never heard about. I was confused and filled with questions with no one to turn to for answers. I knew my parents wouldn't handle the discussion well, and they had isolated me from any other real help.

In addition, I couldn't see any difference between me and the girl on the screen. *If something like that could happen to her, what would prevent it from happening to me?* This thought haunted my thinking as I left the movie. My friend thought the movie was a comedy, so he relived scenes from the movie all night long just to keep the laughter going. I didn't let him know that I was becoming overwhelmed with fear because athletes didn't do that. I went home the next morning deeply shaken.

The next month, I was in agony. I couldn't sleep because of the pictures that filled my mind every time I closed my eyes. I was up five or six times every night, trembling in fear. The only place I knew to turn was the Bible my mom had given me when I was a young boy. I read the Bible just before I went to bed. I slept with it, hoping it would ward off the fear. I read the Bible more each time I awoke in the middle of the night. At the end of that month I was exhausted.

Eventually I found 1 John 4:4: "Greater is he who is in you than he who is in the world" (NASB). The light went on for me. I knew that if somehow I could get Jesus in my life, I would no longer have to be afraid of evil spirits. My brother had made some kind of decision to follow Jesus about three months earlier, so I went to his room and asked him how to become a Christian. He explained to me that I had to admit to Jesus in prayer that I was not good enough on my own to earn salvation. I then needed to thank Him for giving His life on the cross to pay the penalty for all the things I had done wrong. At that point, he told me, I could ask Jesus to come into my heart, and He would spiritually enter my life and give me peace.

That was good enough for me. I went back to my room and prayed just as Jim had told me to. I expected something exciting to happen—to feel different—but nothing appeared to happen. I resigned myself to try to sleep once again. The next morning, I realized I had slept all night without waking up once! Something significant had happened in my life, and I had an instant hunger to figure out what it was. I began reading my Bible intensely. I sought out people at school who could tell me more about knowing Jesus. In college, I joined Campus Crusade for Christ so I could learn how to know Jesus better and help others discover the same privilege.

I came to Jesus because I wanted to be free from the fear that was ruling my life. I didn't realize at the time that He was going to give me a brand-new eternal purpose in life that would help lots of people. I didn't realize He was going to introduce me to a woman who was just as intent on personal growth as I was (Pam and I met while we were involved in Campus Crusade for Christ in college). I didn't realize that God was going to do a new work in Pam's and my life that would break generations of bondage and give our sons a solid start in life. I now believe that someone in my family tree was praying for me. With the hints of a strong spiritual heritage that I have discovered and the effectiveness of the work God has done in both Pam's life and mine, someone must have been praying for decades for a revival in our family.

God obviously had a plan for me (Pam) as well. When I was a preschooler, my mother had a friend named Kathy who was a secretary of a little church in our small town. My mother noticed Kathy had what Mom wanted—peace, joy, and patience. The fruit of the

Spirit emanated from Kathy's life. My mother began to attend Kathy's church and always took us to Sunday school. Mom would then go home, but I would beg to stay for "big church." I felt close to God in that beautiful sanctuary with stained glass windows. And I felt safe.

When I was almost nine, the pastor of the church came to our Sunday school class to ask if anyone wanted to learn more about Jesus. I remember thinking, *Okay, we get Christmas because of this Guy—yeah, I'll go to the class.* In the class, we learned much about who Jesus is, and we also had an opportunity to join a quiz team. Because I always wanted to achieve, I wanted a place on that team! I could just see myself, like a contestant on *Hollywood Squares*, up on that podium, answering those questions. But to win a spot on the team, I had to memorize Matthew 5, 6, and 7.

While reading Matthew, I came across the verse, "Ask and it will be given to you; seek and you will find; knock and the door will be opened to you." I thought, *Does this mean that if I ask You to come into my life, Jesus, You'll do it?* There, sitting on my bed, I bowed my head and prayed, asking Jesus to come into my life to be my Savior, Lord, and best friend. I believe He met me there that day.

I felt free and loved unconditionally. The next day was Sunday, and as was his tradition, my pastor extended an invitation for prayer. I was crying. I remember my pastor asking me, "What's wrong, Pam?" (He did a good job of not rolling his eyes—I was always crying!) I answered him, "I am so happy!"

One day soon after, my best friend asked me if I had a quiet time. I asked, "What is that?" She explained that every day we should read our Bible and pray. So I began to read my Bible and pray. Even though my dad's alcoholism increased, my freedom and joy grew.

However, after our family moved several times, I read my Bible less and less and finally not much at all. Those old perfectionist thoughts returned in my teen years. I thought, *Maybe if I get straight As—then I'll feel loved and accepted. Or, maybe if I become a cheerleader, yeah, that will make me feel loved and accepted. Oh...it must be a college scholarship—that will make me feel worthwhile. Or maybe if I date the coolest guy who drives the coolest car, surely I will feel valuable. If I am the homecoming queen, the crown on my head will make me feel validated, right?* I experienced all those things, and I still felt empty inside! I was looking for love in all the wrong places.

My wake-up call came the day after my brother, sister, and I rescued my dad in the garage. As I drove home from diving practice, I remember hoping my family would realize we couldn't live like that anymore. However, when I walked into the house, nobody wanted to talk about what happened—especially my father, who was a very successful businessman. He was doing paperwork at the kitchen table as if nothing had happened. But something happened to me that day on the drive home—God got in my face. In loving confrontation, God's Spirit whispered to my heart, *Pam, you have been treating Me like your earthly father. You think I am distant, demanding, unrelenting. But I am not like that! Dust off that Bible. Open it up. Find out who I am!*

Shortly after that, a friend, appropriately named Grace, invited me to a Bible study. At that Bible study, I was again encouraged to have a quiet time daily. In one of those quiet times, a few days later, I came across the verse in Romans that says, "By Him we cry, '*Abba*, Father.'" I learned that *Abba* is what Jewish children call their dads when they learn to talk, much like I had said "Daddy." I had a Daddy-God in heaven who loved me! He loved me unconditionally, just for who I was, simply because He created me and wanted a relationship with me! I recommitted my life to Christ, and God transformed me in many ways in a very short time. I quit looking to others to fill my need to feel loved.

As I continued to spend time getting to know God, my freedom returned. I wasn't as driven to achieve, to earn acceptance, love, or significance. Rather, as I felt loved by God, I felt free to be me. As He led me, I excelled—seemingly with less effort. I studied hard and fulfilled my promises simply because those seemed to be the natural things to do. Achievement became a result, a by-product, rather than the key to validation. I exchanged my negative view of my father with a positive view of God as my Father. This gave me the ability to learn to trust trustworthy men. I also learned to respect my earthly father's good attributes (his provision, his great work ethic, his honesty) and not take on the negative ones (his poor self image, his fear of rejection, and his reliance on alcohol). My identity grew from my position with Christ. I knew that I was accepted by God, and I learned to rely upon the Holy Spirit.

It's Not All About the Stats

Statistically speaking, the two of us should not have a great marriage. Daughters of alcoholics tend to marry alcoholics. Sons of paranoid mothers tend to marry women who are chaotic and unpredictable. Those with abusive, angry parents tend to marry abusers. But God had a better destiny for us than that. Somewhere, someone was praying for us, and God heard his or her prayers. Now we have the privilege of helping married couples and families find their own new journeys. Your story is no different. God has been at work in your family. You may be the one to pray for future generations.

> One day a man spotted a lamp by the roadside. He picked it up and rubbed it vigorously, and a genie appeared.
>
> "I'll grant you your fondest wish," the genie said.
>
> The man thought for a moment and then said, "I want a spectacular job—a job that no man has ever attempted to do."
>
> "Poof!" said the genie. "You're a housewife."

Why Did You Do That?

1. How does a person's family impact who they are at work, in social settings, and in volunteer work?

2. How did your family express love when you were young? (Was your home quiet, serene, lively, angry, dramatic, calm, safe, or insane?)

3. Draw a family tree. Write down the people you spent the most time with (aunts, uncles, parents, grandparents). Beside each person's name, list four or five of his or her positive and negative traits.

4. What were the main values your family lived by? Which values do you want to keep, and which ones do you want to reject?

5. What would you like to ask God to redeem in your life?

6. Do you think work settings, social relationships, and church groups can also take on healthy and unhealthy family-like patterns? Explain and give examples.

A man wrapped up in himself makes a very small bundle.
—Benjamin Franklin

The Waffle Warrior

At the beginning of time, "the LORD God formed the man from the dust of the ground and breathed into his nostrils the breath of life, and the man became a living being" (Genesis 2:7). What exactly does being a man mean? A man's untamed heart longs for adventure. He is consistently looking for something in life to overcome. When life is easy, he is bored. When life is too challenging, he is discouraged. He is capable of remarkable feats of strength and courage. He is equally capable of astonishing laziness and neglect.

Driven to Succeed

Men have a built-in drive to succeed. They process life in boxes and evaluate each situation separately. As mentioned in chapter 1, some of these boxes contain areas of life that are very attractive to a man because he knows he can succeed in them. Other boxes are unattractive to him because he doesn't believe he can perform well there. Men only want to spend time in the boxes they are good at. A man who is highly productive at work will enjoy going to work and may even spend too much time there. A man who is adept at athletic competition wants all of it he can fit into his schedule. A man who reads well and thinks clearly is naturally motivated to extend his education. A man who is skilled at making things with his hands will always have a project going.

Unfortunately, this drive to succeed has a dark side. If a man figures out he is very good at unproductive things, he will be just as attracted to them as he is to his positive pursuits. A man who realizes he is good at being lazy will fill his schedule with laziness. A man who constantly hears he is an underachiever will commit himself to underachieve for the rest of his life. If crudeness comes easily and draws laughter and attention, a man will become an expert at being crude. A man whose confidence was shaken early in life can develop a remarkable ability to disappoint people.

In a sarcastic way, Alf Whit captures this dark side of a man's ability to succeed when he says, "I know that somewhere in the universe exists my perfect soul mate—but looking for her is much more difficult than just staying at home and ordering another pizza." In contrast, Steve Mariucci, former head coach of the San Francisco 49ers and now with the Detroit Lions, expresses the intensity of a man who knows he can succeed: "I never wear a watch because I always know it's now—and now is when you should do it."[1]

Untamed Sophistication

When God made man, he made him outside the garden, in the wilderness of life. John Eldredge, in his very insightful book *Wild at Heart*, captures the essence of manhood when he writes, "Adam, if you'll remember, was created outside the Garden, in the wilderness....Man was born in the outback, from the untamed part of creation....Adventure, with all its requisite danger and wildness, is a deeply spiritual longing written into the soul of man."[2] In the heart of every man is the love of adventure. He wants to conquer something, overcome something, discover something, kill something, or invent something. He is never interested in just keeping the status quo. God made him to subdue the earth and cultivate the ground. He is designed to face the wild things of life and bring them under his submission. His most recent victory is never enough to satisfy his soul. He needs a new horizon to discover each and every day of his life.

That is why men are attracted to risk more than their female counterparts. When life is in order and a minimum of effort is required to maintain it, men get bored. This does not appear to be a learned skill but rather an inborn trait of males. "This leads us to one of the very few clear-cut differences in behavior between the two sexes: whenever and wherever they are observed, boys engage in more rough-and-tumble play than girls."[3] For instance, in one study, four-year-old children played on a trampoline in same-sex groups of three.

> About a quarter of the boys engaged in fairly extreme types of horseplay, piling on top of each other on the trampoline or rushing into each other and collapsing in shrieks of laughter. None of the girls played really boisterously, although some of them took part in a more decorous type of high jinks. About a quarter of the girls went to the other extreme, organizing a rotation system in which they went on the trampoline one at a time, while the two other members of the group watched and waited their turn. None of the groups of boys organized such a system.[4]

Putting a ball in the mix is even more interesting.

> In girls' games, the emphasis is usually on keeping the ball going back and forth. The groups of boys, on the other hand, tend to invent rules which ensure plenty of physical contact and an eventual individual winner. Interestingly, this difference between co-operative and competitive styles of playing is greatest between the ages of twelve and fourteen, when concern about gender role is at its peak.[5]

Some adult men are willing to turn anything into a game with a winner. Men like to win at work, and they like to win at play. They like to win at romance, and they like to win at decision making. When they are not the winner, they must recover. They respect those who beat them, but they are always looking for a chance to end up in the winner's circle. Even when they are the spectators, they engage this competitive instinct. When a man who loves sports is watching *his* team win, his testosterone level rises by an average of 20 percent. Likewise, when his team loses, his testosterone level falls by an average of 20 percent.[6] The only conclusion you can reach is that a man feels more like a man when he wins!

Winning Words

Men even have an aggressive approach to conversation. They like to know where the conversation is going at all times. They don't want to control the conversation as much as they want to *succeed* at the conversation. As soon as they recognize something they can talk intelligently about, they jump in before the subject changes. They are easily intimidated by women who can talk about anything at any time. They are amazed at other men who can stay active in conversation. They are even highly critical of them because they don't want to be pressured to be like them. This is a trait that shows up early in life and is only extinguished by the grave.

> Analysis of nursery school children's conversation shows that boys tend to interrupt other speakers nearly twice as often as girls. This establishes a pattern that continues throughout life: at primary school, the ratio of male to female interruptions of a teacher in lessons is very much higher, while in adulthood it has been calculated that men are responsible for no less than 98 percent of all the interruptions that occur in everyday conversation![7]

Related to this phenomenon is the need that boys have to learn from men. Women tend to be more in tune with the developmental needs of their children and are consistently addressing these needs. They read to their children, help their children learn numbers, teach them how to do chores, and so on. But at strategic moments in every boy's life, the voice of a woman will just not do. He must hear from his dad or from some other significant male in his life.

We were vacationing in Hawaii when one of these moments happened in my youngest son's life. Caleb had been watching other children climb a tree, crawl out on a limb, and then jump into the river 30 feet below. The adventure began to lure him. He needed to make the climb and take the jump. His day would not be complete until he conquered this newest obstacle. This was more than fun. This was one of those moments when he would discover how much courage he had. His response to the challenge of the tree could shape his concept of himself for years.

I watched my son as he swam across the river, climbed up the tree, and waited for his turn. Then he shimmied out to the edge of the branch—and froze. He sat motionless, thinking about how high the branch was and how far down he was going to fall. Pam noticed that he had frozen and did her best to help him along.

"It's okay, sweetie. You're safe. Just jump." She was trying her best, but Caleb was not responding.

She tried again, "I am at the bottom, honey. It will be all right. Just let go." Again, nothing.

Then Caleb started to do what no self-respecting boy wants to do. He began to crawl backward off the branch. I knew this was not going to be good for him. The risk of jumping off the tree was not huge. The river's current was slow, no obstacles were in the way, and kids had been successfully jumping all day. In my heart, an alarm went off.

So I separated myself from the rest of the family, and in my most authoritative "dad" voice, I called out, "Caleb." Instantly, he looked at me, motionless. The sound of my voice captured him. I was disappointed for Pam because she had been working hard to help Caleb through this, but her female voice was not working. As soon as I called his name, something changed inside him. His courage seemed to instantly grow, and his back stiffened. I told him to climb back to the end of the branch and listen to my voice. He silently crawled back out and looked once again at me.

I told him, "Caleb, you're thinking about this too much. You already know it will work so I'm going to count to three, and then you jump. Are you ready?"

He nodded his head and looked once more at me. He then looked out as I began to count, "One. Two. Three." He instantly took flight, splashed down into the river, and surfaced triumphantly. He was shouting and whooping it up. He swam over to where I was standing and gave me a high five. I told him I was proud of him, and we hugged each other in celebration of the new victory in his life. For the rest of the vacation, he was more confident, more relaxed, and easier to get along with. The small victory at the river built momentum for victories in other areas of his life.

Meet Me on the Edge

The desire of men to be "dangerous in a safe way"[8] extends to the way we handle money. If our investments are without risk, we are just not interested. If our expenses win us no reward, we get bored with the whole process. When we shop, we want to hunt down our purchases, not graze in the mall. One study reveals that "single women exhibit relatively more risk aversion in financial decision making than single men....Greater financial risk aversion may provide an explanation for women's lower levels of wealth compared with men's."[9]

Men approach every area of life with more risk than their female counterparts. Recent studies have "found that women appear to be less willing to risk being caught and convicted of speeding than men, and that on average women made safer choices than men when it came to making risky consumer decisions, such as smoking behavior, seat-belt use, preventative dental care, and having regular blood pressure checks."[10]

Call Me the Navigator

Studies have now confirmed that men are better at finding their way out of unfamiliar places than women. The most recent research establishes a biological connection. When men navigate their way in a new place, they not only use different parts of their brains but they also only use one side of their brains. Women, on the other hand, have more connections between the two sides of their brains, and they use both sides when making navigational decisions. Even in the car, the waffle and spaghetti distinction holds true. Men approach navigation as a single task and isolate one part of their brain to carry out the task while women connect the two sides of their brain. Men tend to remember directions, such as left and right, while women give directions in relation to landmarks, such as the grocery store.[11]

Men have natural confidence in their ability to find their way. This frustrates those who have to ride with them, as evidenced by the bumper sticker that reads, How Many Roads Must a Man Travel Down Before He Admits He Is Lost? Of course, no man is ever really lost. He just hasn't found his way out yet! To admit he is lost is to admit defeat. He will only admit defeat when the pain of admitting he is lost is less than the pain of continuing the search.

Guys Who Love Movies

When a man and a woman choose a movie to watch, the battle between the sexes lights up. Men like dangerous movies! Men feel "dangerous in a safe way" when they watch a movie that is filled with dangerous scenes and outrageous adventures. The man who wins the woman's heart while defeating the enemy with death-defying stunts is the ultimate man. He overcomes every challenge. We love the hero. James Bond, Superman, Jack Ryan, and Indiana Jones encompass all that we find exciting. Their exploits make us feel as if life is worth pursuing.

Many of us are locked into jobs that lack any sense of adventure. Our lives are filled with responsibilities that must be managed rather than adventures to pursue. We long to find a quest that will capture our heart. We want to climb tall mountains, meet beautiful women who find us fascinating, conquer the evil masters of disaster, and figure out the impossible situation. Our everyday lives don't provide this, so we get lost in movies that take us where we cannot otherwise go.

Most women wish men were more interested in stories of relationships and movies where real-life drama meets character development. But men ask, Where is the danger? Where is the adventure? Where is the impossible situation that will be overcome by the hero of the day? Men wonder, *Why would we want to be entertained by everyday life when it wasn't that exciting the first time?*

Consider Captain James T. Kirk. He makes a habit of boldly going where no man has gone before. If something is out there, he wants to discover it. If obstacles are in his way, he will overcome them. If enemies attack, he will defeat them. If he encounters what seems impossible, he will find a way to make it possible. He is the ultimate warrior.

In *Star Trek III: The Search for Spock,* Kirk is agonizing over his latest decision. Amazingly, Captain Kirk has the ability to show his vulnerability while still being invincible. He engages his good friend Dr. McCoy in a conversation about the latest plight in his life.

Kirk asks, "Bones, what have I done?"

Dr. McCoy fills our hearts with imagination when he reminds his friend, "What you had to do, what you always do: turn death into a fighting chance to live."

In *Star Trek: Generations,* Captain Kirk meets up with Captain Jean-Luc Picard. They will explore together, conquer together, and reaffirm themselves as winners against the forces of evil and mediocrity. In a classic interchange that stirs up everything it means to be a man,

Captain Kirk says, "I take it the odds are against us and the situation is grim."

Captain Jean-Luc Picard responds, "You could say that."

To which Captain James T. Kirk says, "Sounds like fun!"

The Ordinary Adventurer

Indiana Jones is so ordinary, he could be any one of us. He has a responsible job and lives in an average neighborhood. At the same time, he cannot help but find adventures that take him away to exotic places on heroic adventures. That is what every man dreams his life could be. Men who are locked into ordinary, responsible lives long to find the adventure that will convince them they are stronger than life.

Willie Scott is just about overwhelmed in *Indiana Jones and the Temple of Doom* by Dr. Jones' ability to defeat life. In exasperation he says, "You're gonna get killed chasing after your ——— fortune and glory!"

When Indiana Jones responded, "Maybe, but not today," my heart just about leaped out of my chest. In an instant, I knew I wanted to be Dr. Jones and not Willie Scott. I'd love to be able to think up things like this on the spot. In my mind, I know somebody labored over the script to make Indiana sound so spontaneous, but in my heart I want to spontaneously live just like this.

In *Indiana Jones and the Last Crusade*, we admire Sean Connery as Henry Jones, but men long to be his son, Indiana. Henry is the devout, wise, intellectual discoverer. Indiana is the conquering, tenacious, dangerously exciting, fully alive treasure hunter. This difference is clearly displayed in this interaction between father and son.

Henry: "They're trying to kill us!"

Indiana: "I know, Dad!"

Henry: "This is a new experience for me."

Indiana: "It happens to me all the time."

In reality, none of us want to be shot at. We don't want people trying to kill us. We don't want to live on the edge of disaster. But we do want to believe that we could overcome just such challenges if we had to.

The Fantasy Avenger

The other side of the story is just sheer fantasy. We love to entertain thoughts of the impossible. We love to laugh at men in movies who overstate their worth and value. We love to stand with men who overshadow the reality of life. We know the story isn't true, but it transports us to a place in life that is better, more enjoyable, than the stable reality of today. Men don't really want to live in the fantasy of the greatness of the unconquerable male. We just want to visit there often enough to relieve the stress of real life. Consider these bigger-than-life heroes and their bigger-than-life proclamations.

- William Wallace in *Braveheart:* "They may take our lives, but they'll never take our freedom!"

- Colonel Nathan Jessup in *A Few Good Men:* "Son, we live in a world that has walls, and those walls have to be guarded by men with guns. Who's gonna do it? You? You, Lieutenant Weinberg? I have a greater responsibility than you can possibly fathom. You weep for Santiago and you curse the marines. You have that luxury. You have the luxury of not knowing what I know: that Santiago's death, while tragic, probably saved lives. And my existence, while grotesque and incomprehensible to you, saves lives. You don't want the truth because deep down in places you don't talk about at parties, you want me on that wall, you need me on that wall. We use words like honor, code, loyalty. We use these words as the backbone of a life spent defending something. You use them as a punch line. I have neither the time nor the inclination to explain myself to a man who rises and sleeps under the blanket of the very freedom that I provide and then questions the manner in which I provide it. I would rather you just said 'thank you' and went on your way. Otherwise I suggest you pick up a weapon and stand at post."

- Lucilla in *Gladiator,* speaking about Maximus Decimus Meridius: "Today I saw a slave become more powerful than the Emperor of Rome."

  At the climax of the story, Emperor Commodus and Maximus have a showdown that shows the superiority of the gladiator.

  Commodus: "The general who became a slave. The slave who became a gladiator. The gladiator who defied an emperor. Striking story! But now, the people want to know how the story ends. Only a famous death will do. And what could be more glorious than to challenge the Emperor himself in the great arena?"

  Maximus Decimus Meridius: "You would fight me?"

  Commodus: "Why not? Do you think I am afraid?"

  Maximus Decimus Meridius: "I think you've been afraid all your life."

- President Thomas Whitmore in *Independence Day:* "Mankind. That word should have new meaning for all of us today. We can't be consumed by our petty differences anymore. We will be united in our common interest. Perhaps it is fate that today is the Fourth of July, and you will once again be fighting for our freedom. Not from tyranny, oppression, or persecution, but from annihilation. We're fighting for our right to live, to exist! And should we win the day, the Fourth of July will no longer be known as an American holiday but as the day when the world declared in one voice, 'We will not go quietly into the night! We will not vanish without a fight! We're going to live on! We're going to survive! Today, we celebrate our Independence Day!' "

- Ian Malcolm in *Jurassic Park:* "God creates dinosaurs. God destroys dinosaurs. God creates man. Man destroys God. Man creates dinosaurs…"

  Dr. Ellie Sattler: "Dinosaurs eat man. Woman inherits the earth…"

Ahh, the female gender keeps working its way into men's delusions of grandeur. Men like having them around but don't want them spoiling the dream. Men are warriors, and they want women who will pray for them as they go out to battle and hug them when they return from conquering evil. When a woman invades a man's world and tries to redefine it, he gets confused and frustrated.

For instance, in *A League of Their Own*, Tom Hanks, as manager Jimmy Dugan, is feeling the exasperation of women in baseball. He loves the game and is committed to teaching it to his team, but he just can't quite figure out how to communicate to the women. In frustration he blurts out, "Are you crying? Are you crying? There's no *crying* in *baseball!*"

In *The Princess Bride*, Buttercup is afraid and attempts to point out to Westley that the adventure they are on is impossible. She blurts out, "We'll never survive!"

Sensing that she is about to spoil their perfectly dangerous adventure, he assures her in confident ridiculousness, "Nonsense! You're only saying that because no one ever has."

Simply Irresistible

A man's drive to find an adventure he can succeed at creates an intense desire for simplicity. He longs to focus on one box at a time in his life. He wants a manageable schedule and evenly paced expectations. Other boxes are not less important to him. In fact, it is precisely because they are important that he must give them his attention one by one. When he divides his attention, he begins to feel inadequate, and the stress in his life grows.

A man likes to work on one project at a time. He climbs in the box and immerses himself in the project. He forgets everything else in his life and loses himself in the work. When he can work this way, he finds life to be very satisfying. When the project is over, he will stand back and admire his handiwork. He will probably find the people who mean the most to him and ask them to join him in the admiration. Every comment about the beauty of the finished product increases the sense of accomplishment. Every criticism of his work deflates his pride and makes him wonder if it really was worth the effort.

The quickest way to steal motivation from a man is to make him change focus rapidly. This is often confusing to women because they tend to process life in short bursts. They travel the spaghetti noodles of their thought process and actively switch from one subject to another. This makes for a fascinating journey, so women assume that everyone is like this. But men are very different. When a man has to switch subjects quickly, he gets exhausted and confused. He loses sight of what is most important and has a hard time figuring out what needs to be done next. When he can focus on one or two things, he is very productive. But when he has to focus on many things, he can easily become disoriented or frustrated. He will often get angry or just walk away from what looks like a mess to him.

Alec Baldwin gives us ordinary men hope as Jack Ryan in *Hunt for Red October*. He is the hero of the story. He is the one man in the movie who is bigger than life and indestructible. As the plot unfolds, Jack Ryan overcomes every obstacle and figures out every mystery. But he has a simple view of himself. When asked for his identity, his response is simply, "I'm not an agent. I just write books for the CIA." Every man knows that this simple view of his role empowers him to be great. Thinking about every exploit ahead of time creates fear. Reviewing his accomplishments would overwhelm him. When he thinks of himself as a simple author caught in a moment of destiny, he simply overcomes everything in front of him.

This drive for simplicity allows men to boil down the well-being of their lives to one issue. If this issue is good, life is good. If this issue is bad, life is bad.

Searching for Solutions

With projects, men like to work on things that have a solution. A man will lose himself in working on his car because he has a goal and an easily defined finish point. A man will bury himself in his computer because he can always tell when it is working correctly. If something is wrong, he will immerse himself in the solution and spend far too much time working on one problem because he can taste the satisfaction that will result. Having to divert attention from this one project to another disrupts his day. The women who know him don't get it because they think he should just adjust and take care of the simple responsibilities. They don't realize that even the smallest act can disrupt his momentum and throw him off schedule for hours, even days. A man's ability to focus on a single project is a beautiful and highly productive thing. It requires all his energy and consumes his life for the duration. Once the magic is broken, reconnecting him to the task is difficult. He feels ripped off and maybe even lost.

If this happens too often, he may even grow bitter or lazy. He works best when he is able to look to one goal. If he concludes that he will always be interrupted, he will develop a pattern of avoidance. He will despise his laziness, but it will be less painful than pursuing tasks that always get interrupted. On the other hand, he may be driven to accomplish. He assumes that others know how important focus is to him. When others interrupt him, irritation builds up inside him. If specific people in his life are consistently demanding that he switch his focus, he will conclude they either don't know or don't care. If he takes time to explain this to his friend, and the friend continues to downplay his need to stay focused, resentment will build. The resentment will linger until it turns into lingering bitterness. It lurks just under the surface and gets released with each interruption. It surprises him, and it surprises those who get stung by it, but it is very real.

Notice the problem-solving center of this conversation between two men.

> A young woman brings her fiancé home to meet her parents. After dinner, her mother tells her father to find out about the young man, so the father invites the fiancé to his study for a drink.

"So what are your plans?" the father asks the young man.

"I am a Torah scholar," he replies.

"A Torah scholar. Hmmm," the father says. "Admirable, but what will you do to provide a nice house for my daughter?"

"I will study," the young man replies, "and God will provide for us."

"And how will you buy her a beautiful engagement ring?" asks the father.

"I will concentrate on my studies," the young man replies. "God will provide for us."

"And children?" asks the father. "How will you support children?"

"Don't worry, sir. God will provide," replies the fiancé.

The conversation proceeds like this, and each time the father questions, the young idealist insists that God will provide.

Later, the mother asks, "How did it go, honey?"

The father answers, "The bad news is that he has no job and no plans. However, the good news is that he thinks I'm God."

A man, at his best, is refined and wild at the same time. He can be professional and polished while dreaming of the rugged outdoors. He can maintain a responsible life, but he will never be captivated by it. His heart will always yearn for something bigger than life even though he must master the rigors of his daily existence. He is always looking to the horizon. He can be relied upon, but he can never be fully tamed. A man without a dream in his heart is a dead man walking. The boxes on a man's waffle that are filled with adventure and wonder are inconvenient and disconcerting to those who love him the most, but they are what make him a man because they focus his heart. "Above all else, guard your heart, for it is the wellspring of life" (Proverbs 4:23).

The Worth of a Man
In the 1930s, the chemical contents (inorganic compounds) of a 150-pound man were worth $0.98. By the 1960s, the value had increased to $3.50. In the 1970s, the amount had reached $5.60.

The Worth of an Energetic Man
Now, with atomic power in view, this has all changed. The atoms in the human body would produce 11,400,000 kilowatts of power per pound if they could be harnessed. On the basis of this computation, a man weighing 150 pounds is worth $85,500,000,000.

Why Did You Do That?

1. In what areas of life do you feel most successful?

2. Describe what you would consider to be an ideal work day.

3. Do you think men are generally more aggressive and attracted to risk than women are? Explain your answer.

4. What events in your life have been the most powerful in shaping your personality?

5. Do you believe men like to work on one project at a time?

Never believe that a few caring people can't change the world.
For, indeed, that's all who ever have.
—MARGARET MEAD

The Pasta Princess

The Wonder of Women

Fern Nichols was sending her children off to public school, so she met with a friend to pray once a week for the kids and the school. That meeting of two moms wanting to make things better turned into Moms In Touch International, which now has over 20,000 groups meeting in the United States and contacts in 95 countries.

One mom of preschoolers was feeling a little stressed, so she called another mom of preschoolers, and a few friends came together and formed MOPS (Mothers of Preschoolers), which is now over 2700 groups strong in the United States and is represented in 19 other countries as well. Those moms wanted to make things better.

Kay Arthur was teaching a small Bible study for teens. It grew to more and more Bible studies in more and more churches, so she wrote the studies down. Those studies were the start of Precept Ministries International, and they appear in more than 200 languages today. Kay wanted to make life better.

Helen met with some businesswomen for lunch because she wanted to make life better for them, so she taught them about God. Those Christian Women's Clubs grew and spread until Stonecroft Ministries expanded to 14,000 leaders with nearly 2000 clubs.

When my own son entered high school from a small Christian school, I walked onto that campus and thought, *Things need to get better. There are so many broken, hurting students. Too many are on drugs and drinking. Surely I can help prepare Brock to make things better.* I walked alongside Brock as he launched a Fellowship of Christian Athletes club on his campus. I bought pizza as he held team parties to tell teammates how they could come to know God and turn their lives around. I worked behind the scenes, doing practical errands that helped him become team captain in three sports for four years, win student-body offices, and earn the National Football Hall of Fame Scholar, Leader, Athlete Award. I picked up his suit at the cleaners and drove him to the city council to open in prayer. I watched him become San Diego Citizen of the Year. Being "just mom" made things better. I often say, "Girlpower gets things done. When moms get motivated, momentum happens." I think this is true because women want to make things better.

All About Eve

Just as Adam was created outside the garden and longs for adventure, Eve was created inside the garden, and she has her own longings. This was some garden! It was perfect for man to live in.

> The LORD God took the man and put him in the Garden of Eden to work it and take care of it. And the LORD God commanded the man, "You are free to eat from any tree in the garden; but you must not eat from the tree of the knowledge of good and evil, for when you eat of it you will surely die" (Genesis 2:15-17).

It was perfect, except for one thing. Adam was lonely! So God made woman.

The LORD God said, "It is not good for the man to be alone. I will make a helper suitable for him."…But for Adam no suitable helper was found. So the LORD God caused the man to fall into a deep sleep; and while he was sleeping, he took one of the man's ribs and closed up the place with flesh. Then the LORD God made a woman from the rib he had taken out of the man, and he brought her to the man (Genesis 2:18-22).

And Eve got quite the response:

> The man said,
> "This is now bone of my bones
>   and flesh of my flesh;
> she shall be called 'woman,'
>   for she was taken out of man" (Genesis 2:23).

This is the equivalent to a "Oooohhhhh lala!" or "O, baby!" or "Wow, that is some hot mama!" Adam saw Eve and liked what he saw. In a survey of single men, nearly all of them mentioned appreciating the beauty of women. Guys are not deviant for noticing women— God created them that way. Only after the fall of man did this appreciation degenerate into ogling and addictions. Before the fall, as Adam gazed on Eve, everything was good—pure love. My (Pam's) personal opinion is that God gave men a strong sex drive and attraction to women so that when they realize how complicated we women are, they won't say, "I'm outta here!"

> For this reason a man will leave his father and mother and be united to his wife, and they will become one flesh. The man and his wife were both naked, and they felt no shame (Genesis 2:24).

The garden was perfect, God thought Eve was perfect (He made her, after all!), Adam thought Eve was perfect, and even Eve was pleased with herself at first. She must have been—she ran around the garden naked with Adam and felt no shame.

Her Contribution

In the garden, Eve found herself. She knew her contribution. The garden needed tending. However, we can't find any records of bugs or weeds before the fall, so tending was much easier! For Eve, tending the garden was the beautiful (Eve) making more beauty. One of women's greatest roles in life is to express beauty. In one Gallup poll, men said one of the top three things they appreciated about women is that they were well organized.

One advertising survey showed that women's number one desire is for significance. Women want to know their lives count. They want the world to be a better place because they are in it. Emotionally healthy women intrinsically desire to leave the world better than they found it. They want people to be glad they were there.

Her Compassion

In the survey we conducted when preparing *Single Men Are Like Waffles, Single Women Are Like Spaghetti*, the quality that single men found most attractive about women was their relational skill. They used many different words to describe it (kind, tender, empathetic, loving, nurturing, sweet, nice, a good listener), but all the descriptions can be summarized in one word: compassion. Waffle warriors appreciate that somehow women love them!

Her Character

And lest we forget, Eve was made in God's image. God possesses all the qualities of both males and females (and then some!). We are reflections of Him. That is some great DNA! In addition, women were created from the rib of Adam. Some wedding ceremonies include these words that describe the significance of Eve's original creation:

The woman God made was not taken from man's head to rule over him, nor from under his feet to be trampled upon by him, but from his side that she might be his equal, from under his arm that she might receive his protection, and from near his heart that she might own and command his love.

What character strengths does a woman commonly display?

- *Her ability to read between people's emotional lines.* Because women are often more skilled at expressing emotions, they typically read other's emotions better than most men do. If your mom, sister, wife, or daughter says, "Maybe you need to talk to someone," or "You should make things right," or "Can you find out what is going on with so-and-so?" then you should probably at least consider the request. She might be seeing into a person's heart or reading his or her body language.

- *Her intuition.* A woman can see with her feelings. If she says, "I'm uncomfortable with this," "I'm not sure about this," "Can we pray about this?" or "I feel really great about this opportunity! I think we should go for it," her intuition might be a real lifesaver!

- *Her ability to nurture.* Studies have shown that higher testosterone levels are associated with people (men and women) not hearing a baby's cry as well or as quickly! Some biology is behind all that nurturing, mothering stuff. If you feel at all uncomfortable with your relational skills or your parenting qualities, then ask the most nurturing woman in your world to mentor you. Your wife, sister, or mom might give you some clues on how to better relate to your coworker, your toddler, or your teen.

When Good Intentions Go Bad

Women who see their contribution, compassion, and character as good become women of influence, women who feel significant. Women do make a difference! Only as they fall prey to the lies of Satan and become discontent do they experience trouble. Eve was living out her destiny and had a terrific self-image—then things changed:

> Now the serpent was more crafty than any of the wild animals the LORD God had made. He said to the woman, "Did God really say, 'You must not eat from any tree in the garden'?"
>
> The woman said to the serpent, "We may eat fruit from the trees in the garden, but God did say, 'You must not eat fruit from the tree that is in the middle of the garden, and you must not touch it, or you will die.' "
>
> "You will not surely die," the serpent said to the woman. "For God knows that when you eat of it your eyes will be opened, and you will be like God, knowing good and evil."
>
> When the woman saw that the fruit of the tree was good for food and pleasing to the eye, and also desirable for gaining wisdom, she took some and ate it. She also gave some to her husband, who was with her, and he ate it (Genesis 3:1-6).

The serpent told her that if she ate, her eyes would be opened and she'd be like God. Eve was discontent. She didn't think she was good enough as she was. She wanted to be better. And most men do not appreciate that self-depreciation. Many males in our survey said they hated hearing women put themselves down.

In one focus group, Brad said, "I hate hearing women put themselves down. It's a real slam to the guy they are with—as if he doesn't have good taste being with her. I'm attracted to a woman who has confidence in herself."

Eve should have been confident. Check out God's take on creation:

> So God created man in his own image, in the image of
> God he created him; male and female he created them....
> God saw all that he had made, and it was very good (Genesis
> 1:27,31).

After all the other days of creation, the Bible says, "And God saw that it was *good*." But after creating man and woman, God said it was *very good*.

Eve thought she could improve what God created. Eve wanted control. She wanted to be her own god. What were the results?

> Then the eyes of both of them were opened, and they
> realized they were naked; so they sewed fig leaves together
> and made coverings for themselves (Genesis 3:7).

The first result is *shame*. She felt bad about herself—so bad that she covered up her body. Those fig leaves were the original "fat clothes." (Guys, all women have fat clothes. They are the clothes they wear when they are feeling bloated, ugly, and fat. These clothes are often worn during PMS. They are usually baggy and drab, and they come with matching accessories, such as a carton of Ben and Jerry's Chocolate Fudge Brownie ice cream.)

Then Adam and Eve acted ashamed and made some bad relational statements:

> Then the man and his wife heard the sound of the LORD
> God as he was walking in the garden in the cool of the day,
> and they hid from the LORD God among the trees of the
> garden. But the LORD God called to the man, "Where are you?"
> He answered, "I heard you in the garden, and I was afraid
> because I was naked; so I hid."

> And he said, "Who told you that you were naked? Have you eaten from the tree that I commanded you not to eat from?"
>
> The man said, "The woman you put here with me—she gave me some fruit from the tree, and I ate it."
>
> Then the LORD God said to the woman, "What is this you have done?"
>
> The woman said, "The serpent deceived me, and I ate" (Genesis 3:8-13).

Studies have shown that when men fail, they blame some outside circumstance. Here, Adam started it. He blames Eve—*and God* for giving Eve to him. Now *that* is a cop-out! Few things irk a woman more than men who won't step up to the plate and accept their responsibility. Guys who are willing to say, "I'm sorry" or "I blew it. Please forgive me," will always have the best relationships with women. At one conference, a man handed us an article with the headline, "Men Who Say 'Yes, Dear' Have Better Marriages." The headline was a bit misleading, but the main point of the article was that men who are willing to agree with women have better relationships with them. This should be a no-brainer, but some men still are unwilling to admit they are wrong. Everything that goes wrong in a relationship becomes the woman's fault. When a guy maintains he is always right, he might protect his ego and pride, but he will be very lonely because any self-respecting woman won't want anything to do with him!

But Eve wasn't much better. She made her own choice without regarding the consequences. And the consequences were substantial:

> To the woman [God] said,
>
> "I will greatly increase your pains in childbearing;
>   with pain you will give birth to children.
> Your desire will be for your husband,
>   and he will rule over you."

To Adam he said, "Because you listened to your wife and ate from the tree about which I commanded you, 'You must not eat of it,'

> "Cursed is the ground because of you;
>> through painful toil you will eat of it
>> all the days of your life.
> It will produce thorns and thistles for you,
>> and you will eat the plants of the field.
> By the sweat of your brow
>> you will eat your food."

Adam named his wife Eve, because she would become the mother of all the living (Genesis 3:16-20).

Eve became the mother of all living, but because of her discontent and desire to control, she had pain in childbearing—and so do all women. I picture a long line in heaven as women complain to Eve about PMS, periods, and menopause, and they recount their own pain in childbearing. *Thanks, Eve!*

And in addition to pain in childbearing, the text says: "Your desire will be for your husband, and he will rule over you."

No, gals, this doesn't mean that you will have some hot, flaming, erotic desire for the man you marry (although that is good!). Rather, theologians explain this verse to mean we will desire our husband's role, but men will "rule" over us or be responsible for leading. Adam didn't step up to be a leader in the garden. He knew the fruit was off-limits. But he wasn't effective in passing God's command along to Eve, and when she disobeyed, he went right along with her. Like Eve, Adam believed Satan instead of God. He also didn't keep Eve's best interests in mind.

Let's look closer at the results of the fall. The whole childbirth process is in place because of menstruation, which begins for most girls between the ages of 12 and 14 and ends with menopause between the ages of 48 and 58. So that's 34 to 46 years of monthly cycles, bloating, cramps, and feminine hygiene products. Then, factor in PMS, which is an official malady (not something that's just in a woman's head). We try to cope with the mood swings and pain of PMS by joking about it. You've probably heard a few jokes like these:

> Question: What is the difference between a woman in PMS and
>   a terrorist?
> Answer: You can negotiate with a terrorist.
>
> Question: What is the difference between a woman in PMS and
>   a pit bull?
> Answer: Lipstick.

The first part of the curse is pretty well accepted. Childbirth hurts. I can personally attest to this! However the second part of the curse gives women a much tougher time in life. The propensity to be discontented, to control life, can be the ruin of many a good relationship.

When Estrogen Goes Awry

I have often thought that we need to start a support group for recovering control freaks and perfectionists. You know, *Control Freaks Anonymous*. However, it would probably never get off the ground because each of us thinks he or she should be the one in charge!

Since the Garden of Eden, women have had this problem of wanting control. "My way or the highway." I (Pam) am convinced that as a result of the curse, we women have control issues. We naturally want to rule the universe. We tend to think our ideas are best even when we have no moral or ethical reason to think so. We still want control. If you think I'm kidding, just take a day and watch how often women, especially at home or in a comfortable work environment, second-guess men. How often does your own mother say, "Why did you do that?" or "No, that's not the way it was, remember?" And then she goes on to correct someone in front of family or friends. And how often do women criticize men for their methodology? Watch an evening of sitcoms and count how often the dad of the show is put down. Just because men do things differently than a women doesn't make them inferior or stupid.

Open Season on Males

Male bashing is popular in our culture. Attacking males seems to be one of the few slams that aren't politically incorrect. This is open season on males. Check out a few greeting card lines I saw recently:

Menopause, menstruation, mental illness, premenstrual syndrome. See? All of our problems go back to men.

I even found a website with over 100 male-bashing jokes. Here are just a few:

Question: What should you give a man who has everything?
Answer: A woman to show him how to work it.

Question: What do you call a man with half a brain?
Answer: Gifted.

Question: What is gross stupidity?
Answer: 144 men in one room.

Question: How many men does it take to pop popcorn?
Answer: Three. One to hold the pan and two others to a c t macho and shake the stove.

Question: How many men does it take to change a roll of toilet paper?
Answer: Who knows? Did it ever happen?

Question: What is a man's idea of doing housework?
Answer: Lifting his legs so you can vacuum.

Question: How do you get a man to do sit-ups?
Answer: Put the remote control between his toes.

Question: Why is psychoanalysis quicker for men than for
    women?
Answer: When it's time to go back to childhood, he's
    already there.

Question: Why is that only 10 percent of men go to
    heaven?
Answer: If all men went, it would be hell.

Need more evidence that we women might have an attitude?

In one set of surveys we took, we asked both genders to share the trait they appreciated most in the opposite gender. In a group of nearly 100, less than 50 women could name *even one* trait they appreciated about men. Most of the surveys came back blank on just that one question! On the other hand, nearly every man had numerous traits listed that they appreciated in women. Are men inferior? Definitely not! Have women been trained to undervalue the contributions of men? Or have our experiences with a few men jaded our view of all men?

Our Heroes!

Like many other people, Bill and I were horrified as we learned of the deaths of the nearly 400 would-be rescuers at the World Trade Center disaster. We realized that the majority of these brave heroes were men. The passengers who overpowered the hijackers on flight 93 were men. Throughout history, men have been doing heroic things and saving countless lives. We thought about the soldiers sent away to Afghanistan to find Osama bin Laden. They too were mostly men. And those serving for freedom in the gulf? Mostly men. With one of our sons already registered with Selective Service and another one due to register next year, we are reminded once again to be grateful for "the guys."

What Women Want

Some women in our survey did appreciate traits of men. Number one was a man's strength and protection, and second was his ability to cope or step back and be objective.

Gals, we can't have it both ways. We can't want men to be just like us and also expect them to step up and step in to do the hard, dirty work of rescuing those in danger. That's not fair! God created them with testosterone so they would be prepared to provide and protect.

If we find ourselves with a chip on our shoulder toward men, we each need to take responsibility to figure out why it's there. We each need to ask strategic questions of ourselves: Was it trained into me? Was I hurt or misused by a male in my life? Was I abandoned or abused by a male authority figure? Then we need to take the next step and do something to correct the pain that is causing the attitude. Some corrective options include...

- *counseling* to remove the pain
- *complimenting* males to retrain our minds
- *caring* for the males in our world to build a more healthy emotional response

Sometimes guys just don't know what we want. They're in a double bind.

> If you work too hard, you never have any time for her.
> If you don't work enough, you're a good-for-nothing bum.

If she has a boring, repetitive job with low pay, it's exploitation.

If you have a boring, repetitive job with low pay, you should quit being so lazy and find something better.

If you get a promotion ahead of her, it's favoritism.
If she gets a job ahead of you, it's equal opportunity.

If you mention how nice she looks, it's sexual harassment.
If you keep quiet, it's male indifference.

If you cry, you're a wimp.
If you don't, you're insensitive.

If you make a decision without consulting her, you're a chauvinist.
If she makes a decision without consulting you, she's a liberated woman.

If you ask her to do something she doesn't enjoy, that's domination.
If she asks you, it's a favor.

If you try to keep yourself in shape, you're vain.
If you don't, you're a slob.

If you buy her flowers, you're after something.
If you don't, you're not thoughtful.

Do we women set men up to fail?

The Princess and the Pea

When I was little, one of my favorite television specials was "The Princess and the Pea." A traveler came into the kingdom, and she needed a place to sleep out of the cold weather. The king placed her in the nicest room with the nicest mattress. She couldn't get comfortable, so he commanded his servants to add another mattress. Still the traveler couldn't get comfortable. Over and over again they added mattresses, and still the young woman tossed and turned all night. In the morning, as the servants removed the mattresses, one found the tiniest little pea. Upon learning this, the king and queen quickly realized the traveler must be a princess, a perfect match for their own prince of a son.

This is a fairy tale, but for the prince it was the beginning of a nightmare—the "nothing is good enough" nightmare. Women who have been the center of their daddy's world, who were doted upon while not being asked to bear a growing level of responsibility, can be high maintenance. Nothing will be as good as Daddy did it. A woman who thinks this way may have a difficult time bonding to a man because all men live in the shadow of her doting daddy. She may also have been spoiled, so she may expect royal treatment. She may feel manicures, massages, and memberships to prestigious clubs are each a must, a right, a requirement rather than a privilege or perk.

If you were told over and over while growing up that you were "Daddy's little princess," you might actually begin to think you are the center of the universe and the sun should rise and fall upon your whims. Well-meaning parents of either gender can foster an unhealthy self-love in a child. Or, if you were ignored or unfairly criticized as a child, you may have an overstated need for attention as an adult.

One teen, while at a friend's for dinner, wanted all the attention on her. Whenever the conversation would drift from her as the family chatted around the table, she would announce, "Focus, focus! Back to me." This was amusing at a dinner party, although not to her mother! Most women are not this bold, but I have observed that women raised as "princesses" like attention and will try to control circumstances when they feel the focus is drifting from themselves or their agenda.

Another young woman told Bill in a premarital counseling session, "We don't want to have kids. I am the princess of the family. I am the only daughter, the only granddaughter, and the only niece. I have been the center of attention of my family, and I like it that way."

Bill turned to her fiancé and said, "Are you okay with this?"

The fiancé nodded sheepishly.

Bill looked him square in the face and said, "Man-to-man—I want you to remember this years from now when she wants all your attention. When she wants the world to revolve around her needs and not yours. Just remember, this trait is not likely to ever change. You knew about it, you accepted it, and you asked for this. Remember, you wanted it."

Some women will desire and manipulate until they get all the attention, and others will constantly create a crisis. These women should wear the T-shirts that say, "Drama Queen." Some women will do anything to be the center of attention, even create a crisis if need be. Love, to them, is a soap opera.

The Soap Opera Syndrome

The "soap opera syndrome" develops in a home with a lot of conflict. Kids in these homes correlate conflict with love. Nothing feels like love unless it includes a little bit of pain. The trouble with being a drama queen is that not many kings want that kind of constant crisis. Most men want to know life will be easier, not harder, if they date you. If a guy is constantly on pins and needles, wondering if the smallest comment will set you off, you will have a quick turnover of men in your life. Or you will get in a long-term relationship with a man with whom you can carry on a lifestyle of conflict.

Women often ask, "Why do I attract all the losers? If I walk into a room with 100 great men, I'll find the one loser of the bunch!" I often refer to this as the "loser magnet" or the uncanny ability to attract unhealthy men. It's common among women who have been victimized. Subconsciously they think they don't deserve to be treated well.

Shonda traced her princess syndrome back to an unhealthy father who spoiled her but was untrustworthy because of his alcoholism. At college, she submerged herself in a women's studies program with professors who consistently promoted women and demeaned men. She married Bill right out of college and soon found herself discontented with everything he did. She told him what lane to drive in and how much butter to put on his toast. She questioned his parenting decisions and corrected him in front of company.

"I was ruining our relationship with my control," she told me. "After the second baby, I was just out of sorts. I wish I could blame my attitude on baby blues or my hormones, but I had developed a pattern to harp, complain, nag, and criticize. Bill tried everything to appease me. One day he exploded. Escaping to the peace of our garage, he slammed the door just after he shouted, 'Will you ever be happy?'

"That was the first time I asked myself the same thing, *Would I?* I was married to a man who loved me and the children, provided well, attended church with me, and I never thanked or praised him—or at least rarely did. No wonder I felt a distance growing between us."

We women must realize early in life that we are *not* in control. Life will always be imperfect.

Life Feels Out of Control

All women, single and married, go through a midlife transition between the ages of 28 and 38. We ask, *Who am I? Why am I here on earth? What do I do with this ticking biological clock?*

Midlife can feel very uncomfortable for a woman. She may feel like her choices are out of her control. She longs for more. If she doesn't pursue answers to these questions through Bible study, small group interactions, mentors, and time with God, her personal pain draws her into other, less healthy activities. She may become depressed. She might have suppressed anger expressed through a sharp tongue or a sarcastic wit.

Some women develop a cynical view of their role with men. "Men are like fine wine. They all start out like grapes, and women need to stomp on them and keep them in the dark until they mature into something you'd like to have dinner with."

Some of these women give up on men entirely, either turning to lesbian relationships or just becoming male bashers. Other women try to "fix" men, which leaves them "looking for losers." As some people say, a woman marries a man hoping he will change, and he doesn't. A man marries a woman hoping she will never change, and she does.

A woman can develop a role as a rescuer. If she hasn't married, she may look to a man to help define her, thinking if she were married she'd be happy, or at least happier. She may hear the biological clock ticking and be willing to take any man so she can have a baby. This can lead to a desperate decision.

Catherine explains, "My friend, Trish, who married a neighborhood jerk we both grew up with, asked me recently, 'Isn't your mother worried about you?'

"I replied, 'Why would my mom be worried about me?'

"'Well, you're 30 and not married. Is something wrong?'

"'Nothing's wrong with me. If any mom should be worried, it should be your mom. Tom doesn't treat you very well, and now you have two kids to take care of. I don't want to settle because I didn't take time to discover who I was and expected a guy to fill me in!'"

Some women want to feel life is under control, so they give up control of their lives to a man.

"My friend Jenny is a mystery," said Kristine. "She was a successful career girl, making close to six figures a year. She had a house and a new car. Then she met Jared. She sold her house and her car. Suddenly he has a house that's being remodeled, and he has a new sports car. Jenny has nothing. She even quit her job! What is that? And for what? She's been living with Jared for nearly six years without a ring. He is such a jerk. He even jokes about it. He said to me, 'Did you hear? I have a surprise for Jenny.'

"'Wow, are you finally going to propose?'

"Then Jenny walked up and he started laughing. Jenny said, 'Oh, is he joking about asking me to marry him?'"

Kristine looked at me and said, "How can a woman stay with a man who would joke about something as tender as that? Why stay with a jerk? I don't think he'll ever ask her. Years from now he'll just get a younger version, and then where will Jenny be? She'll have no home, no car, no job, no money, no life."

Kevin sees this as a major issue in the women he has dated. "The women get too dependent. They start asking my opinion on everything. I don't know. It's not my life. I like a woman who is more confident and self-assured—someone who has some sense of herself."

No One's Going to Tell Me What to Do!

Other women swing entirely the other direction and refuse to trust men they can't control. We see a pattern of women who marry milquetoast men because they are easy to control. Then, as they travel through life and the responsibilities of life build, these same women become angry that their men don't step up to the plate. They marry a spineless man and then suddenly expect him to show some backbone when life gets challenging.

From my experience ministering to women, I believe more than half of all women fall into this category. A woman is wounded growing up, so she decides she will never relinquish control of her life. She meets a man who doesn't mind her emasculating him with constant correction, criticism, and control. She wears the pants in the relationship. They marry and have children, and her way is always the right way. This system may work for a few years until—*bam!* A crisis happens that she can't control. Suddenly, the crisis becomes *his* fault because he can't fix it. But he either can't or won't fix it because she has never allowed him to fix anything. He pulls further and further away from her, and he becomes more and more passive. She helped create this passive man, and now she resents him for being that way.

The signs of a dominating, controlling female show up early in a relationship. Do you see any of these early warning signs?

1. She throws an emotional tantrum if he doesn't give her enough time or spend enough money on her.

2. She belittles or corrects him in public.

3. She takes on too many responsibilities too early in the relationship.

4. She demands lots of phone calls and make lots of phone calls.

5. She is jealous of his time commitments: his work, his friends, his family.

6. She always wants the details of his plans.

7. She becomes angry at surprises.

8. She forces him to choose her over his friends.

9. She tells people how they should think and feel.

10. She isolates him from past relationships.

Pack Your Bags, We're Going on a Guilt Trip

Some women give over control, and others learn to manipulate to control. By keeping the guy they are with off balance emotionally, these women control the power in the relationship. Men consistently report they are bothered with women who read too much into every statement, action, or nonaction on their part. These men never know whether they are on solid ground or in the doghouse. Every day seems to have a new set of rules. Guys get weary of always feeling "wrong." Pouting and crying might work for a moment, but they rarely work for a long-term relationship.

Your security as a woman has to be in Christ, not in a man. No man will be able to read your mind and tell you what you want to hear. No man will know when he did or said something that hurt you. No man will be able to protect you from every hurt and inconvenience. To expect a guy to come running when you feel panicked, hurt, frustrated, or just plain moody is unrealistic. And if you do manage to weather a turbulent dating life, your spouse probably won't be able to meet the unrealistic expectations you will place on him in marriage.

He may get discouraged and angry and leave. Or he may withdraw because you will constantly make him feel like a failure. He will tire of the hysteria, and he'll escape to safer emotional ground.

What are some signs to look for that may signal you are a woman with unreal expectations?

- *Do you expect him to know how you are feeling?* Don't do this! Explain your feelings using "I" statements, such as, "When you said that, I felt devalued. You might not have meant it that way, but I thought I should tell you."

- *Do you expect him to keep you from harm?*

- *Do you expect him to come running if you hit a crisis or snag?*

- *Do you expect him to cater to you?*

Some single guys are perceptive and spot the princess syndrome quickly. Single women can tip their hand. One man said, "When she picked lint off my shoulder and told me to tuck in my shirt, I knew I had to end the relationship."

Many a good man will run from a woman who thinks she must be the center of attention. Consider the couple in this joke:

> In her own eyes, Julia was the most popular girl around.
> "A lot of men are gonna be totally miserable when I marry."
> "Really?" said her date, "And just how many men are you intending to marry?"

As we learned earlier in the book, men like to go to boxes they can succeed in. If a man feels like he isn't a success around you, he may not want to stay with you. He will feel like a constant failure in your eyes. Men have difficulty staying motivated in a relationship when they feel inadequate.

Coming to grips with the possibility that you may be a pasta princess is difficult. Ask yourself these questions:

- Did my father abandon me physically?
- Did he abandon me emotionally? (Was he an alcoholic, drug addict, or workaholic? Was he emotionally distant or unavailable?)
- Was I abused mentally, emotionally, physically, or sexually?
- Was I the center of attention?
- Did I usually get my way while growing up?

If you answered yes to even one of these questions, your chances of being a pasta princess are pretty high.

If you felt abandoned as a child, you may want control so you won't ever feel abandoned or emotionally let down again. You may wonder if you can trust men. You feel you can trust yourself, so you want control. If you have been abused, you might have some well-founded trust issues, so you will have to rebuild a circle of trustworthy males into your life.

Seeking professional counseling will help you recover and restore your ability to spot a trustworthy male. If you are single and keep dating men who mistreat you, you may have a problem. It's not just the men you date. Women who have been victimized do not behave and act in the same way as do women who have not been wounded. They tend to maintain the "victim" role. Counseling helps a woman recover from her wounds, become more confident in Christ, and be more centered as a person. Men who are victimizers no longer find her attractive.

How can you find good counsel that will help you overcome these trust issues and remove the "jerk magnet" from your life? The following items are not just for single women but for all women who want to reach their God-given potential. Good counsel will help you take these three steps toward a healthier life:

Discover your identity in Christ. As you see yourself and your life from God's point of view, you will begin to value yourself more. As you value yourself more, you will not put up with abuses of any kind from men. Also, you won't need to control as much because you will gain comfort from God's loving character and His control of you and your life. In surrender to God's love and His sovereign control, you will be freed from thinking you have to be the god of your little world. Trying to control your world will shrink your world down to a size you can control—and that is pretty small. However, releasing control to God expands your world and thus expands the opportunities God can bring your way.

Identify the core issue. By discovering why you fear failure, have a hard time releasing control, mistrust men, or choose unhealthy men, you will grow in areas that were shut down emotionally. Abuse often stops the growth process. For example, if you were sexually abused at 16, you may only be able to relate intimately to men on the level of a 16-year-old. You might be making decisions in this very adult area of your life with the emotional skills and viewpoint of a 16-year-old, regardless of your true age. The Bible encourages us to grow in grace, to come to maturity in Christ (2 Peter 3:18). Good counsel will help you identify core issues so you can grow in those areas.

One woman who came to our office had been hurt by a series of bad choices of men she had allowed into her life. At 16 she had been date raped. At 18 she married a drug addict and then got divorced. At 20 she remarried to a gambler who spent all her money, and they divorced. At 26 she moved in with a man who ended up beating her whenever he drank, and he drank often. Then at 29 she married a man she met during a prison ministry. He vowed he had changed and promised her the moon, but he abandoned her when he was released. When we met her, she said, "No more! I don't have the time or energy for another bad relationship. I want to have a relationship, but I want to know what I am doing to attract all these unreliable men!" Good girl!

She is well on her way to having the ability to find healthy men attractive.

Develop new tools. Good counsel will provide you with new resources and tools to better equip you for healthy relationships. A counselor's goal should be to strengthen you so you don't need to come and see him or her anymore. Expect counseling to be hard. Look at it as a college course for life. Prepare to read many books, practice new skills, and pray through barriers so you can grow.

Pasta princesses can either hang on to that ugly control freak inside and drive people away, or they can make things better by giving control of their heart to God's loving care and find compassion, character, and their unique contribution. In this way, they can become "Queen of Quite a Lot" because people of both genders will be drawn to their influence.

Top Ten Reasons Why God Created Eve

10. God worried that Adam would always be lost in the garden because men hate to ask for directions.

9. God knew that Adam would one day need someone to hand him the television remote.

8. God knew that Adam would never buy a new fig leaf when the seat of his wore out, and he would therefore need Eve to get one for him.

7. God knew that Adam would never make a doctor's appointment for himself.

6. God knew that Adam would never remember which night was garbage night.

5. God knew that men would never be able to handle childbearing.

4. As keeper of the garden, Adam would never remember where he put his tools.

3. The scriptural account indicates Adam needed someone to blame his troubles on when God caught him hiding in the garden.

2. As the Bible says, "It is not good for man to be alone!" And the number one reason why God created Eve...

1. When God finished the creation of Adam, He stepped back, scratched His head, and said, "I can do better than that."

Why Did You Do That?

1. Men, compliment a woman in your life on one aspect of her character, one example of her contribution, or one demonstration of her compassion.

2. Women, communicate to a man in your life one piece of information that you learned about the "control freak" in most women. How does what you learned impact your life?

3. What issues from your past could impact your future as a spouse? What is one change that you want to make to correct a misconception or counter the effects of a bad choice?

4. Do you think the women you know receive respect and honor for their contributions, compassion, and character?

5. What changes can women make to better help men understand them and work with them?

6. How can a man point out to a woman that she may have control issues without offending her?

7. What resources, professionals, or other people might help you navigate personal change?

You shall know the truth, and the truth shall make you mad.
—ALDUOUS HUXLEY

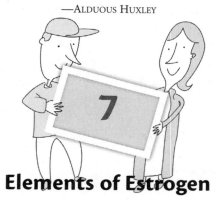

Elements of Estrogen

Janet is a creative and energetic mom. She is a successful real estate agent and is actively involved in her community. Her kids are used to depending on her, and their school has come to rely on her competent volunteer efforts. Her friends have always complimented her for being able to juggle many responsibilites with skill.

Janet was disheartened when she realized she was becoming moody and depressed. Because she had some good days, she was able to hide her sadness from most people. Whenever her husband and kids worried about her, she bounced back and became the woman they loved so much.

One day, her family noticed she was especially anxious in the morning when they left for work and school. The tension continued to grow as each of them arrived home that afternoon.

"How are you doing today, Janet?" her husband asked innocently.

Janet erupted, "Can't you tell how I am? I am miserable. All I ever do is give, give, give. All you ever do is take, take, take. How am I doing? Well, take this!"

At that, she threw a plate across the room, and it shattered. Janet finally decided to see her doctor. A full battery of blood tests and chemical studies revealed that she had...premenstrual syndrome (PMS).

The research on PMS is still controversial.

One reason why the premenstrual syndrome is so controversial is that researchers do not agree upon the definition of the syndrome....Another reason why premenstrual syndrome is so controversial is that some experts claim that all menstruating women experience it, because they all have cyclic variations in their hormones. Other experts maintain that premenstrual syndrome is a myth—"It's all in their heads." Neither of these views does credit to women. The first view stresses that we are almost entirely at the mercy of our hormones. Feminists are concerned that people who overemphasize the premenstrual syndrome are out to make a "fast buck" on therapy sessions and medications. The second view is equally unfair to women because it ignores the fact that some women do experience more tension premenstrually than at other times in their cycle.[1]

A review of the research reveals that up to 150 different symptoms are associated with PMS. Most of the symptoms are relatively minor, but the effects are sometimes so severe that a woman cannot work or carry on normal activities for a brief period of time. PMS usually begins a week or two before menstruation and continues until a woman's period begins. Common symptoms include headaches, depression, moodiness, fatigue, breast tenderness, fluid retention, backache, cramps, acne, weight gain, swelling, constipation, allergies, and joint pain.

PMS—Who Can I Blame?

We would like to blame it all on Eve and the forbidden fruit she ate in the garden. PMS definitely is related to the ability to bear children and all those delightful hormones. Most researchers agree that it has to do with an imbalance of hormones during the second half of a woman's menstrual cycle. In a normal cycle, levels of estrogen (which stimulates the growth of the uterine lining, among other things) in your blood rise until ovulation. Then they decline, and progesterone (which causes the lining to thicken) levels begin to rise. If your body is producing and metabolizing the right amounts of estrogen and progesterone at the right times, you won't get PMS. However, vitamin deficiencies, emotional pressure, or any number of other stressors can upset the delicate system, and that equals PMS.

Medical experts provide lists of symptoms of PMS, but some of the prevailing humor captures the heart and essence of PMS in a much more practical way.

How do you know if you're experiencing PMS?

1. Everyone around you has an attitude problem.

2. You're adding chocolate chips to your cheese omelet.

3. The dryer shrunk every pair of your jeans.

4. Your husband is suddenly agreeing to everything you say.

5. You're using your cellular phone to dial the number on every bumper sticker that says, "How's my driving? Call 1-800———."

6. Everyone's head looks like an invitation to batting practice.

7. You're counting down the days until menopause.

8. You're sure that everyone is scheming to drive you crazy.

9. The ibuprofen bottle you bought yesterday is empty.

You know a woman has PMS when....

1. She stops reading *Glamour* and starts reading *Guns & Ammo.*

2. She considers chocolate a major food group.

3. She's developed a new talent for spinning her head around in 360-degree circles.

4. She retains more water than Lake Superior.

5. She denies she's in a bad mood as she pops a clip into her semiautomatic and "chambers one."

6. She buys you a new T-shirt with a bull's-eye on the front.

7. You ask her to please pass the salt at the dinner table, and she says, "All I ever do is give, give, give! *Am I supposed to do everything?*"

8. She enrolls in the Lizzie Borden School of Charm.

9. She orders three Big Macs, four large fries, a bucket of Chicken McNuggets, and then mauls the manager because he's out of Diet Coke.

Why PMS?

What is really going on in a woman's body that seems to "send" her? PMS is most likely caused by a combination of things—hormone, chemical, or nutritional imbalances. It may be an imbalance of the sex hormones estrogen and progesterone that causes PMS. Too much estrogen can make you anxious, irritable, and confused. Too much progesterone, a natural relaxant, can lead to depression. Other experts argue that low blood sugar plays a role in PMS. During the premenstrual phase, levels of glucose, or blood sugar, may drop. Low glucose can cause headaches, depression, and confusion. A concerted research effort has revealed much about PMS:

- Estrogen levels generally rise and progesterone levels drop roughly one week before the onset of menstruation.

- A B$_6$ deficiency prevents the liver from processing estrogen efficiently, resulting in bloating, weight gain, and tenderness of the breasts.

- Fluctuations occur in serotonin, impacting a woman's sense of well-being.

- Fluctuations occur in melatonin, affecting a woman's sleep pattern.

Foods that make the impact of PMS worse are white sugar, white flour, caffeine, alcohol, and foods high in fat content.

Cramping Your Style

"For women who are made miserable each month by cramps, it may seem outrageous that many doctors consider them to be a minor complaint. Their financial impact certainly isn't minor: They cost companies about 140 million lost work hours each year," says Lark. Cramps are just one of the many PMS symptoms that may make life more difficult.

A woman's body is in a constant state of flux. Our opinion is that PMS is real, but a woman doesn't have to be ruled by her hormones. And PMS shouldn't be used as an excuse for antisocial or hurtful behavior. In one study, college students were asked to respond to a variety of excuses given for antisocial behavior. In general, premenstrual and menstrual excuses were not looked upon negatively.[2] A consequence of this acceptance of PMS as an excuse is that women may not take appropriate responsibility for bad choices and bad behaviors. One mother of a grown son relayed the following story to me:

> I am glad my son, Pete, came in to see Bill for counsel-
> ing. His fiancée was out of control. Nothing was ever right
> or good enough. She'd act poorly and then blame PMS. One
> day my son said, "Mom, this can't really be PMS, can it? She
> blames PMS almost every day for almost everything. It's not
> possible to have PMS everyday, every month, every year, year
> after year, is it?"

After he talked with his mom and then Bill, he ended the engagement. No one likes an unkind, controlling, always-stressed person—
PMS or not. We women can't always blame our choices on PMS
without demeaning real PMS symptoms or the severe PMS that other
women may really have to deal with. We must not be like the boy
who cried wolf. If we cry PMS too often, we will lose the sympathy
of those around us. People have little patience with women who never
take responsibility for their actions and choices. Use PMS excuses sparingly. When you really do need an extra dose of compassion, you are
more likely to get it.

Empathy and small gestures of care really do help. Husbands can
use a small dose of TLC to help lower the tension when their wives
experience PMS. "Reassurance and understanding that this isn't all
in your head goes a long way to help relieve PMS," says Dr. Steven R.
Goldstein, professor of obstetrics and gynecology at New York
University. "There is a physiological reason you feel the way you do.
It's not just a fluffy diagnosis."

Please Help Me!

For some women, the ten days to two weeks before their period
starts has a Jekyll-and-Hyde effect on them. Most doctors recommend
that you keep a symptom chart so you have an accurate record of the
emotional and physical changes affecting your life. Mark the days
on a calendar that you don't feel your best. Also note things like
bloating, headache, and anxiety. Rating your symptoms may also be

informative. For example, a headache could range from one to ten in intensity. Your anxiety could be rated from one for a little grumpy to ten for "I feel like I am totally out of control and want to hurt someone!"

Keep a record for two or three months to see if symptoms cluster around your period. If you're experiencing PMS, your discomfort should occur during the two weeks before your period and go away after your period starts.

Charts can be powerful tools. I (Bill) began to notice about ten years ago that Pam was getting more headaches than usual. Coincidentally, I also saw her transform from the encouraging cheerleader I married to a woman who was sometimes anxious, irritable, and bossy. After a few months, I thought I could see a trend, so I began to record the days she was "different." Once I recorded four months, we were amazed to see that the headaches were 28 days apart. Pam was thinking they were caused by stress or the rising responsibilities in her life, but the problem was PMS. She met with her doctor shortly after that and began to deliberately chart her cycle. She has now learned to recognize the difference between hormone headaches, stress headaches, and just plain life pains. Much to my relief, we have learned to predict her bouts with PMS. I can give her grace when I know that she isn't upset because of something I did wrong.

PMS remedies are ongoing areas of study. The results aren't conclusive, but based on anecdotal evidence, changes in diet, exercise, and relaxation can greatly reduce symptoms. Each woman should take personal responsibility in discovering just what remedies help her the most. Every woman has a different hormonal system, so what works for your friend may not make you feel better at all.

From All Sides

Battles are often won by attacking the enemy from all sides. The battle against PMS is no different. You are created with a mind, body, and spirit. The remedies we choose should consider nutrition, exercise, stress reduction, medicine, and dietary supplements. But I have found great help looking beyond myself for strength and power. On those days I feel just awful, I remember a few things that help me behave in a way that my friends and family can handle.

Perspective: I remind myself that millions of people in the world are in real pain. War, famine, disease, and poverty are serious problems. PMS is mostly just an inconvenience. On my worst PMS days, I read biographies of women who have endured and overcome much, such as the pioneer women who traveled the Oregon Trail. These women gave birth, only to see their babies die and then bury them in the path of the wagon wheels. As the wagons traveled over the grave, the dirt would be compacted and wild animals couldn't dig up the bodies. That is real trauma. That is real pain. PMS is a distraction, a discomfort, and maybe a source of temporary depression, but it isn't disaster. On PMS days I send cards to friends with cancer. I e-mail a friend who has just lost her husband or child. I refuse to sit around feeling sorry for myself, regardless of how lousy I feel physically. I choose to do something for someone in real pain. I get my eyes off myself.

Priorities: But I am also a realist. On the second day of my period, I always feel like I have the flu. Everything aches. My head feels like someone put it in one of those football helmets with air cushions but they pumped it too full. My entire head feels like it is in a vise grip. I give myself some slack. I am not as creative on those days, but I can still do simple tasks: editing, research, housework, organizing, delegating. If I want to, I take a short nap, go for a walk, or swim. I have noticed which exercises and activities seem to lessen the physical symptoms, and I add them in to my schedule on peak PMS days, even if I must set aside some "vital" issue for a day or two.

Prayer: I ask God to fill me with His spirit of love, joy, peace, patience, kindness, goodness, faithfulness, gentleness, and self-control. When I feel I'm at the end of myself, I ask God to send His strength in the areas I feel weak. I pray, *God, I feel like I want to snap everyone's head off. Give me Your patience today. Please don't let me take out my pain on others. Instead, God, give me kindness in my answers, give me grace when responding, and give me love above all no matter what the kids or Bill say or do. Let me choose to express love. I don't have it in me on my own, but since Your Spirit lives in me, I know I can draw upon Your power to do the right thing. Help me, Jesus.*

And help me He does. I always try to keep in mind that other people aren't at fault simply because their request or need falls on a day I feel so needy myself. I don't want to say or do anything during PMS or during my period that I have to spend the rest of the month making up for! God's power is big enough to meet all the needs if I allow His strengths to flow through me.

Pampering: I take life and its responsibilities down a few notches. I exercise, take a nap, get a massage, or take a bubble bath. If I have to carry a full load that day, I make those around me aware of what I am dealing with. For example, I will explain to the boys, "Guys, you know how you feel after two-a-day football practices? Well, that's how I feel today. I'd be more than glad to spend the day running errands for you, but I am wondering, can any of them wait until tomorrow when I'll be feeling better?" Sometimes they can, sometimes they can't. If the list can't wait, then I make a deal—I get to choose the music on the radio. They might not like the harp music, but they are glad they get to go shopping. Life is full of compromises.

Prepare: Most of the rest of this chapter explains what PMS is and includes practical ways to handle it. God wants us to seek out the truth and then use it. He set certain patterns into place, and the health professionals, scientists, and mental health community are discovering the truth about what God has done. Preparation is vitally important. One woman I know became desperately depressed for a few days each month. Her husband just couldn't understand her severe mood swings. One day she'd look and feel like a model, and the next she was so self-loathing she might cut herself or try to overdose on pills. He began to notice the frequency of these episodes were approximately the same distance apart—a month. He persuaded her to go to a PMS clinic, where she learned how to adjust her diet and activities. He got his wife back. She will still be a little melancholy a few days a month, but his fear of walking in and finding her the victim of a self-inflicted wound is gone. She has prepared herself for victory over PMS.

What's on Your Plate?

Nutrition plays a role in PMS. Saturated fats (red meat, cheese, and butter) can raise "bad" prostaglandin levels, producing uterine discomfort, bloating, and mood swings. Sugar and caffeine deplete all the B vitamins and some minerals, including chromium. Caffeine has been directly linked to breast tenderness. Alcohol interferes with the liver's ability to process excess estrogen.[3] Easing your PMS symptoms might be as simple as monitoring when and what you eat. Consider some of these dietary tips gathered from a variety of PMS specialists:

Eat often. During PMS, many women have low blood sugar. When blood sugar drops, cortisol is released, making you feel nervous, jittery, and anxious. As blood sugar plummets, you crave cookies, chips, and just about anything fried in grease.

> Women with PMS crave sweets, which creates a vicious cycle: Sugar depletes magnesium, which in turn kindles sugar cravings. Sugary and salty foods also aggravate bloating and breast tenderness, and sugar depletes B-complex vitamins, increasing anxiety and muscle tension.[4]

If you eat at least every four hours, you will be more likely to make wise choices. Most doctors recommend eating three small meals and two to three snacks a day.

Choose slow-burning foods. Pick foods that your body processes slowly. Lean protein, such as chicken, turkey, soy foods, and fish, and above-the-ground vegetables, such as broccoli, cauliflower, and peppers, are all good choices. Try not to eat foods that can raise blood sugar quickly, such as white flour, white sugar, potatoes, and carrots.

Choose complex carbs. Because carbohydrates raise serotonin levels, women's sugar cravings in the second half of their cycles are an instinctive attempt to feel better. Beans and whole grains, such as millet, oats, and rice are always healthy choices because they are high in magnesium, a natural tranquilizer that relaxes muscle contractions; potassium, which reduces bloating; and fiber, which also helps remove extra fluid from the body. In addition, these complex carbohydrates help stabilize blood sugar levels, which will decrease your cravings. A good rule of thumb is to look for brown foods at the grocery or health-food store: brown rice, oatmeal, and whole wheat. Eat whole foods (grains, fruits, vegetables, soy foods, beans, nuts, and seeds) and reduce or eliminate junk food (processed food, sugar, caffeine, soda, and alcohol). Use dairy products sparingly, if at all; they can interfere with magnesium absorption, and magnesium lessens uterine cramping.

Enjoy fruits and vegetables. Besides being good sources of fiber, many of these are high in magnesium, potassium, and calcium, another nutrient that acts as a mood relaxant. A lot of fruits and veggies are also rich in vitamin C, which helps get nutrients into tight muscles and helps alleviate stress. Rama Kant Mishra, a physician and researcher, suggests drinking plenty of warm water, and eating coconut, raisins, papaya, and sweet juicy fruits.

Skip salt. Salt encourages your body to retain water, which can cause bloating all over your body. Water retained in the brain can cause headaches, and extra water in the breasts can make them tender.

Kick caffeine and alcohol. Soft drinks are packed with sugar. Alcohol is processed into sugar by your body, and it depresses your nervous system, which affects mood. Women who drink alcohol often complain of anger as a PMS symptom. The caffeine in your morning coffee or afternoon soda can cause breast tenderness, mood swings, and anxiety. Though they may seem to stimulate your energy or help you relax, caffeine and alcohol actually work against you.

Drink water! Instead of coffee or soda, guzzle water. Some women fear that drinking more water will add to bloating, but adding water helps your body eliminate fluids. When you're dehydrated, your body hangs onto water, making bloating worse.

A Smorgasbord of Supplements

I noticed that in my thirties, my lunch conversations with girl-friends seemed to change. "I got this great new herb tea at the health food store. You should try it. Really helps with PMS." We went from swapping recipes for the family dinner to recipes for natural concoc-tions to help us want to even be with our family! When stopping by most any of my friends' homes, I am sure to spot at least one ency-clopedia of herbs or homeopathic natural remedies.

Opinions vary about which supplements and natural remedies might give some relief. Supplements are very controversial in medi-cine and research. They are not as regulated by the FDA as drugs are, and many patients are resistant to telling their medical doctors about the supplements and other natural remedies they may be using. But patients should never withhold information from their health professionals. Here's a sampling of supplements:

Vitamins: In addition to the right food and drink, some vitamins, minerals, and supplements have given women relief. A study of more than 400 women in the *Journal of Obstetrics and Gynecology* found that 1200 milligrams of calcium supplement each day cut PMS symp-toms almost in half after three months. The B-complex vitamins, which are involved in more biochemical reactions in the body than any other vitamin, seem to improve mood and reduce bloating. To help soothe nerves, some women take magnesium.[5]

Natural hormones: As women age, they tend to lose progesterone before estrogen. (Progesterone is made from the egg that's released every month, and women ovulate less regularly as they age.) As a result, the impact of PMS is likely to increase with age.

Restoring progesterone in the second half of the cycle can relieve many symptoms, but caution is in order. There are many forms of both synthetic and natural progesterone, and they produce different effects for different women. In addition, advances are continually being made, so a straightforward discussion with your physician is a wise move to determine which path is best for you.

Other herbs: Herbalists often formulate a PMS herbal treatment program based on a woman's particular cluster of symptoms. Evening primrose oil and other essential fatty acids, such as borage or flaxseed oil, are sometimes recommended by doctors to reduce cramping and relieve breast tenderness. All are sold at most health food stores.[6] Evening primrose oil can be very helpful in alleviating PMS. In one study, women who took the herbal oil experienced a 60 to 70 percent reduction in PMS symptoms over a five-month period.[7]

Four oils—evening primrose, borage, flaxseed, and pumpkin seed—contain an essential fatty acid that is converted to a "good" prostaglandin in the body. They are available in capsules in natural food stores. You can also use one tablespoon of flaxseed oil in salad dressing.

Chaste tree berry *(vitex agnus castus)* is one of the best-researched herbs for women. German studies show it stimulates progesterone production and may regulate estrogen as well. Nearly 60 percent of the women in a 1987 study at a London PMS clinic said chaste tree berry relieved all or most of their symptoms, particularly anxiety, nervous tension, insomnia, and mood swings. And a 1979 study showed it to be helpful in relieving water retention.

Black cohosh root *(cimicifuga racemosa)*, which contains phytoestrogens, was an official drug in the United States Pharmacopeia from 1820 to 1926. In a 1982 double-blind study of 80 women in Germany, it relieved hot flashes, headaches, joint pain, sleep disturbances, and depression better than synthetic estrogen. Those with a heavy menstrual flow and pregnant women should discuss taking black cohosh with their health practitioner because it can increase flow.

Dong quai *(angelica sinensis)* is one of the most widely prescribed Chinese herbs for PMS. Because it contains phytoestrogens, it's a good hormone balancer. It also calms uterine cramps and relieves pain.

For cramps, those who believe in natural remedies suggest that you drink a cup or two of red raspberry leaf tea. For bloating, drink a cup or two of dandelion tea. (If you have cramps and bloating, you can drink both teas!)

Rub it in! Herbal educator and aromatherapist Penny King of Georgetown, Texas, suggests a simple and relaxing massage oil to relieve cramping, bloating, and lower back pain. Pour some unscented lotion or massage oil into the palm of your hand. Add one or two drops of the essential oil of clary sage, chamomile, geranium, lavender, or orange blossom. Massage the mixture into your aching abdomen and lower back.

Commonsense Solutions

Some of the best steps you can take to control PMS include habits that can improve the general health of either gender.

Shed some light on the problem. When you don't feel well, you sometimes want to isolate yourself. Fatigue and mild depression may tempt you to find a dark corner where you can try to hide from life until you feel better. Getting into the light can have an amazing influence on your attitude, your energy level, and your general well-being. Take a walk in the sun. Sit in front of your largest window and enjoy the scenery. Go to a public place where the lights are bright. Don't let your mood determine the brightness of the day.

Work up a sweat. Doctors don't know for sure why exercise helps PMS, but some believe that it helps stabilize blood sugar. Getting active may also increase endorphins, the body's relaxing hormones that are 500 times more potent than morphine. A brisk 20- or 30-minute walk three times a week seems to be enough to help most women. Exercise is one of the first things that the staff at PMS Access in Madison, Wisconsin, recommends to the more than 2000 women who call every day with questions on how to relieve PMS naturally. Cofounder Marla Ahlgrimm, a registered pharmacist, says exercising helps women elevate their mood and ease anxiety.

Exercise reduces stress, raises serotonin levels, increases oxygen in the blood, and improves the blood flow, which helps reduce water retention. By strengthening muscles, it can prevent lower back pain and cramps. Any aerobic activity—walking, swimming, bicycling, tennis, or moderate jogging—will make you feel better and give your body an advantage over PMS. I work out three times a week, but I increase the activity the week before my symptoms usually begin. Studies show that women who engage in regular exercise—30 minutes of walking or aerobics at least three times a week—report milder symptoms, says Valerie Montgomery Rice, a reproductive endocrinologist at Henry Ford Hospital's Division of Reproductive Medicine in Detroit.[8]

Relax. Go for the obvious—get away from the stress! Run a hot bath and soak for 20 minutes, or walk the dog around the block without the kids. Most women can clear their heads in 15 to 20 minutes by themselves. A once-a-month massage therapy session might be worth the investment if it brings you serenity, sanity, and stress relief so you can continue to cope. In addition, peaceful music, such as hymns played on a harp, string quartets, or praise music can help you relax, especially if it includes truths that remind you that God cares for you and that God is still in control. Try all these by candlelight, especially candles that emit your favorite scent as they burn!

Remember that the solution to your PMS pain must agree with Scripture. For example, many women's magazines encourage meditation to lower stress. But the Eastern religious practice of emptying your mind opens the door for Satan to fill it. A biblical view of meditation is found in Philippians 4:8. "Finally...whatever is true, whatever is noble, whatever is right, whatever is pure, whatever is lovely, whatever is admirable—if anything is excellent or praiseworthy—think about such things." Instead of emptying my mind, I focus on God or good things given by God as I rest with my eyes closed or swim laps in the pool. For example, each time I swim, I either list God's attributes from A to Z, or I mentally recite a praise chorus that lists His traits. These exercises remind me of all that God is and that He is available to help me through this tough place. Hold every idea up to the light of truth. The Bible says, "You shall know the truth and the truth will set you free."

Beyond Self-Help

Matt called frantically. "Bill, what do I do? Cammie is so out of control. She was so angry she just pulled a knife on me! I don't want to call the police—she is a wonderful woman. You mentioned at our last session that this violence might be PMS induced, and I think you're right. I need to get her some specialized medical and emotional help. What was that number you gave me?" Sometimes diet and exercise don't even come close to fixing the problem. Specialized medical treatment from an expert in PMS is sometimes the best and most expedient choice. Get on the Internet and find out which hospitals and clinics specialize in the treatment of women and PMS.

Your doctor might suggest a low-dose birth control pill. The pill can regulate your menstrual cycle and keep your hormone levels steady throughout the month. New hormone-based drugs are always being developed.

> For severe PMS, some doctors prescribe antidepressant medications such as Prozac and Zoloft, which increase serotonin levels. A recent study found that women with PMS have fewer emotional problems while taking Zoloft. These drugs may cause nervousness, insomnia, nausea, and diminished libido, however, so work with your physician to find the best product and dosage for you.[9]

Prescription drugs to alleviate PMS symptoms is a controversial topic in many theological circles. Some churches see it as a sin, others see it as a practical solution. Each woman needs to search the Scriptures for herself and pray, asking God to confirm the path she needs to take in order to...

- *Save her life.* A dead witness is no witness at all. If you are severely depressed and are a harm to yourself or others, drastic help is needed.

- *Save her relationships.* Keep working toward a solution that is the least invasive to your body and maintains your most vital relationships.

- *Save her witness.* The fruit of the spirit is love, joy, peace, patience, kindness…so if you have erratic mood swings that hurt your Christian witness in the workplace or community, you need to continue seeking solutions.

PMS or Perimenopause?

Many women notice that their PMS gets worse with age. Some people believe that this is related to the hormonal changes that happen prior to menopause. As the body prepares to shut down its reproduction cycle, it produces less and less estrogen and progesterone.

Women usually experience menopause between the ages of 49 and 54, but women can be in perimenopause for as long as 10 years before menopause. "Menopause is really ovarian retirement," explains Dr. Christine Green, a family physician in Palo Alto, California. "But the ovaries don't quit all at once, they just go on vacation."[10]

On the Bright Side...

Hang in there, ladies. Keep experimenting to find what lowers the stress during those PMS days. Buck up, guys, and keep it in perspective—PMS is only *temporary*. Men, don't take everything she says so personally on those days. Give her a break with some empathy. How happy are you when you have the flu, a headache, or cramps of any kind? Take something off her plate one day a month. Take the kids to the movies or the park for a few hours. You'll be pleasantly surprised at the results of a little TLC.

Ladies, ask God to help you lower the stress and to make better choices in words and actions despite how you feel. Men have bad days (for other reasons), and we expect them to be kind. Here's the dialogue that goes on in my mind: *God, right now I am feeling stress. I feel (angry, stressed, teary) and right now I need Your help to make a wise choice.*

Give me Your strength, Your power to do what is right regardless of my
feelings. Thank You that the fruit of the Spirit is love, joy, peace, patience,
kindness, goodness, faithfulness, gentleness, and self-control. I choose now
to be empowered by Your Spirit. Amen.

This doesn't mean I always make the right choices, but every time
I pray that prayer, God is faithful to come through with help. An easier
prayer to start might be, "God, help me want help. Give me the want
to, to want to!"

In addition, God would want us women to make good, healthy
choices for ourselves. By seeking out wise choices in food, exercise,
supplements, medicines, and supportive relationships, we are loving
ourselves as God would. In turn, as we take good care of ourselves,
we'll take better care of our responsibilities and relationships. God
wants what is best for us and our lives. We need to take responsibility for seeking out what is best for us.

" 'My patients today do not have to wait years, as I did, to see their
symptoms disappear,' Lark writes in her book. 'Most of them feel
remarkably better in one to three months.' "[11]

"However you treat your PMS, remember you're not alone. 'Find
a person who believes that what's going on with you is real,' says
Michelle Blum. 'I thought I was going crazy before. Now, I feel like
I'm in control.' "[12]

Recently, Bill and I took a huge step of faith financially for our
organization, Masterful Living. I was feeling more stress than normal,
and a friend picked up on it. I e-mailed her a "thanks for asking" and
asked her to pray for me, adding, "On top of this huge financial step
for Masterful Living, I am experiencing PMS." She e-mailed back,
"PMS = Pre Masterful Living Success." I smiled. In combating PMS,
nothing beats a good friend praying and a good sense of humor!

Question: How many women with PMS does it take to screw in
a light bulb?

Answer: One. *One!* And do you know *why* it only takes *one?* Because no one else in this house knows *how* to change a light bulb. They don't even know the bulb is *burned out.* They would sit in this house in the dark for *three days* before they figured it out. And once they figured it out they wouldn't be able to find the light bulbs despite the fact that they've been in the *same cupboard* for the past *17 years.* But if they did, by some miracle, find the light bulbs, *two days later* the chair that they dragged from two rooms over to stand on to change the *stupid* light bulb would *still* be in the *same spot!* And underneath it would be the *crumpled wrapper* the *stupid light bulbs* came in. *Why?* Because *no one* in this house *ever* carries out the *garbage!* It's a *wonder* we haven't all *suffocated* from the piles of *garbage* that are *12 feet deep* throughout the *entire house.* The house! *The house!* It would take an *army* to clean this *house...*

Why Did You Do That?

1. Women, on a scale of one to ten, how would you rate your stress during PMS? Men, what did you learn that made you more empathetic of the women in your life?

2. How should a coworker handle a woman in PMS? Ignore her? Accommodate her? Keep the same standards? Lower the bar? Acknowledge the PMS? How can someone be empathetic yet not patronizing of a woman experiencing PMS and menstrual symptoms?

3. Should businesses, the government, or the military acknowledge PMS or menstruation in any policy?

To change and to change for the better are two different things.
—GERMAN PROVERB

Change—The Only Constant
for a Woman
(How's a Guy Supposed to Handle It?)

I (Pam) admit it. I am a woman over 40. And after 40, a woman's life—especially her body—changes. After I turned 40, my arms suddenly grew so short that I couldn't read the phone book very well. The print was irritatingly small. So I got bifocals. One of my friends knew that I was a little distraught over this new age marker in my life, so she zipped off the following e-mail to me (in 18-point font size).

Pam,

Welcome to the ranks of the perimenopausal. Life will be changing, but don't worry. Arm yourself with a good sense of humor, and you'll be fine. After all, in today's world, all kinds of things are changing (see attached).

Love,
Menopausal and making it.

What was attached? "Even Barbie's Changing."

> *Bifocals Barbie:* Comes with her own set of blended-lens fashion frames in six wild colors (half-frames too!), neck chain, and large-print editions of *Vogue* and *Martha Stewart Living.*
>
> *Hot Flash Barbie:* Press Barbie's bellybutton and watch her face turn beet red while tiny drops of perspiration appear on her forehead! With handheld fan and tiny tissues.
>
> *Facial Hair Barbie:* See Barbie's whiskers grow! Available with teensy tweezers and magnifying mirror.
>
> *Cook's Arms Barbie:* Hide Barbie's droopy triceps with these new, roomier-sleeved gowns. Good news on the tummy front, too: muumuus are back! Cellulite cream and loofah sponge optional.
>
> *No More Wrinkles Barbie:* Erase those pesky crow's feet and lip lines with a tube of Skin Sparkle Spackle from Barbie's own line of exclusive age-blasting cosmetics.
>
> *Midlife Crisis Barbie:* It's time to ditch Ken. Barbie needs a change, and Bruce (her personal trainer) is just what the doctor ordered. Comes with Prozac. They're hopping in her new red Miata and heading for the Napa Valley to open a B&B. Also comes with real tape of "Breaking Up Is Hard to Do."
>
> *Divorce Barbie:* This one comes with Ken's car, Ken's house, and Ken's boat!

Obviously, these are all a joke. Mattel isn't changing their doll. But, Doll, we are changing, and only a good sense of humor will get us through!

Ever-Changing You!

Women and their hormones make constant *changes*. Change is such a part of being a female that one of our main transitions in life is affectionately called "The Change." Yes, perimenopause and menopause are synonyms for the word *change*. One researcher describes the chaos of perimenopause this way:

> Mood swings? Perimenopause is the period of time two to seven years prior to the cessation of your periods. Characterized by hot flashes, weight gain, mood swings and energy, menstrual, and sleep pattern fluctuations—and a general desire to snap anyone's head off at any time of day.[1]

But you think we women would be accustomed to change by now. Think back. Life, hormones, and emotions are fairly stable in a little girl's life. But womanhood is a different journey altogether. Just about the time we are ready to give up the backyard swing, we exchange it for an emotional swing and menstruation. For some girls, puberty begins as young as nine or ten, but most girls experience puberty between the ages of eleven and thirteen. We spend our teen years trying to stabilize the erratic emotions that spring up once a month. Usually we have learned enough coping skills to eventually convince some guy that he wants to marry us.

Then what happens? Pregnancy! Your husband may wonder what happened to the sweet wife who once sat beside him, stroking his forehead and listening to his problems. He might wonder, *Where is the woman who used to love to cook me meals or rub my neck after a hard day? Who is this woman who now screams or cries at the drop of a hat and sends me out for pickles or ice cream? Who is this woman who whines at the size of her growing belly and constantly asks if I'll rub her swollen feet? She even sets me up in a no-win situation by asking, "Am I fat?"*

But praise God that in the middle of pregnancy, your hormones do you a favor and, in spite of the size of your tummy, your libido kicks into high gear, and your husband never looked so good! You enjoy a few weeks of chasing him around the house and increasing the pace of your sex life. And then, just as suddenly, about the time he is really enjoying this stage of pregnancy, your hormones shift again, and you can't even imagine wanting to take off your caftan-like muumuu for sex or any other reason. This frustration peaks during the transitional phase of delivery with a tribal-like shriek: "Look what you did to me!" Fortunately, that anger is short-lived, and the new baby welcomes you into a new state of happiness—except that many women fall prey to baby blues or postpartum depression. Eventually, our hormones return to their normal spontaneity and we adjust to motherhood.

The Midlife Moment

These drastic changes—PMS, pregnancy, postpartum, and stabilization—repeat themselves with every child we bear. Then, sometime during our childbearing years, usually between the ages of 28 and 38, when we get a moment to reflect, a midlife transition hits. For some women this is a great time of clarification. For others it is a huge jumble. The transition includes questions such as Why am I here? and What is my purpose in life? During this time, each woman discovers the fullness of her purpose on earth. Her goals as a mother come into focus. The direction of her career picks up passion. The contribution she will make to her generation starts to take shape. She may feel like she is melting down, but she comes out the other side with golden wisdom in her hands, and she knows what she must do with the best years of her life.

Just about the time we figure ourselves out, we are greeted by perimenopause and menopause. Our lives get thrust into another roller coaster of change that dominates our emotions. Finally, after menopause, if we are fortunate, our hormone levels stabilize. With enough TLC, supplements, medication, and family understanding, we can enjoy a semi-sane last leg of life. So only at the very beginning of life, when we are too young to appreciate it, and at the end of life, when we are too old to do much with it, are we emotionally stable!

That means women must *embrace change* as a friend. If we see it as an enemy, change will get the better of us and defeat us. Biology does affect us, but it doesn't have to enslave us! Change is easier to embrace if we know what to expect and what might help us manage it. The only constant in a woman's life is change, so we'd best learn to use it for our good instead of letting it get the best of us. Let's get the best from change!

A (Sometimes) Welcome Change

Women often look forward to pregnancy. But with each pregnancy, women need God's perspective on the new little bundle of joy that has been placed in their womb. The psalmist writes,

> Sons are a heritage from the LORD,
>   children a reward from him.
> Like arrows in the hands of a warrior
>   are sons born in one's youth.
> Blessed is the man
>   whose quiver is full of them (Psalm 127:3-5).

Regardless of the timing, God's point of view is that children always have value. They are always a blessing. But we women don't always feel blessed. Morning sickness that lasts all day, a tiredness that won't go away, indigestion, weight gain, bloating, back pain, and one look in the mirror, and we can feel anything but blessed! To manage the constant changes of being female, gather great info. Go after the facts of what the next transition may be like. If you know what to expect, then you'll say, "Okay, this is normal. This is temporary. I know how to handle this." If you fail to prepare, you prepare to fail. Facing the transitions of womanhood without guidance is comparable to setting out to cross the Mojave desert on foot with no sunscreen or water. However, if you have a mentor and some good books about the coming transitions, you will survive and maybe even thrive through them.

Guy to Guy

Keep this in mind, men. Whatever changes your wife is going through—PMS, pregnancy, perimenoapuse, or menopause—you are going to be right there with her! Her issues become your issues. Sorry, that's just the reality of marriage. Here are a few hints that will help:

Get informed. Learn everything you can about the issue at hand. I went to all Pam's doctor's visits each time she was pregnant, and surprisingly, I really enjoyed learning all about what was happening to her and our children in utero. Because I had done my homework and been at all the doctor appointments, the doctor ushered me into the operating room, breaking hospital policy, when Pam had to undergo an emergency C-section. Because I had been supportive of Pam, I had the joy and rush of seeing Brock's exciting birth and the doctors' lifesaving work. Sharing and caring equals connection to a woman, and when she feels emotionally connected to you, she will want to be physically connected to you as well.

Get a grip. Women's emotions are volatile—erratic at times—and you cannot ride the roller coaster with her. Her bad mood doesn't have to put you in a bad mood. Just keep doing what is right and normal, and give her some space. If she is a spiritual woman and has a connection with God, God will whisper to her, *You overreacted. Go apologize.* Don't feel compelled to point out all her mood swings and seemingly irrational thought patterns and behaviors. The most loving thing to say may be, "Honey, why don't you let me take the kids." Or "Sweetie, why don't I just handle this for you. Why don't you just go out shopping (or take a bubble bath, go work out, or call a friend)?"

Get in sync. Sure, she will be going through many changes. But you will also have some rough terrain to traverse. After having a couple kids, you may face a "fight or flight" decision. You might feel being married is too hard, being a dad is too tough. Chickens and cowards run, but real men stay and fight for their marriage and family. They decide to hang tough and be a hero to their wife and kids.

You may also hit what Pam and I call the "Superman" phase of life. Providing for your family will take all your focus. This is admirable, but don't leave your family behind. Keep in touch. Keep a date night with your wife weekly. Take time out for your children. No man at the end of his life has said, "I wish I had spent more time at the office."

Don't miss out on some of the best memories of your life by being preoccupied with work.

Get stabilized. Her changes and emotions can set off your unresolved issues and old baggage. Resolve to be a mature man. Get a mentor. Meet in a men's Bible study. Learn how to pray alone, with and for your wife. The number one request we get when speaking to women is: "How can I get my husband to pray with and for me?" It doesn't have to be fancy. Just wrap your arms around her daily, or reach over and hold her hand and pray something as simple as,"God, thank you for my wife. Encourage her." She didn't marry Billy Graham. She married you, and your voice praying for her is like music to her soul. (A note: Couples that pray together daily rate their sex life at the highest possible rating. Are you motivated?)

A Major Adjustment

Pregnancy is a huge transition for a marriage. It's full of excitement, new beginnings, hopes, and dreams. But it's also full of emotions. What happens to a woman's emotions during pregnancy? *What to Expect When You're Expecting* lists a woman's emotional changes in each month of pregnancy:

Months One Through Three
>   Instability, including irritability, mood swings, irrationality, weepiness
>   Misgivings, fear, joy, elation—any or all of these

Months Four Through Six
>   Joy and apprehension (if you have started to look and feel pregnant)
>   Frustration from being in-between. Your regular wardrobe doesn't fit anymore, but you're not looking pregnant enough for maternity clothes.

Feeling as if you're not quite together. You're scattered and
forgetful; you drop things and have trouble concentrating.

Fewer mood swings but occasional weepiness and irritability

Continued absentmindedness

Boredom with pregnancy

Anxiety about the future

Months Seven Through Nine

Increasing excitement

Increasing apprehension about motherhood, the baby's
health, labor, and delivery

Increased dreaming and fantasizing about the baby

Increased boredom and weariness with the pregnancy, or a
sense of contentment and well-being, particularly if you
are feeling great physically

Increasing eagerness for the pregnancy to be over

Increased absentmindedness

Excitement—along with a little anxiety—at the realization that
it won't be long

Relief that you're almost there

Irritability and over-sensitivity (especially with people who
keep saying "Are you still around?")

Impatience and restlessness[2]

Men Have Feelings Too

Guys whose wives are expecting can feel overwhelmed, excited, and
sometimes neglected. With all the attention on the wife, husbands have
to choose to not feel left out. Wives can help by continuing to romance
their husbands and treat them with respect. Wives should assume they
want to be good dads and trust them to be equal parenting partners.
They may not do everything the way their wives would, but *different*
doesn't mean *wrong*. Tami Chelew, founder of Wives in Prayer, says,

"Sometimes we (the wife) have to step back so he (the husband) can step up."

Feeling Blue after the Baby

In addition to the emotional changes during pregnancy, many women are also prone to some form of the blues after the birth of their child. Depression in general is more common in women than in men, particularly women in their primary reproductive years (25 to 45). Your reproductive status and your susceptibility are obviously linked, as depression is more common during the premenstrual phase, the perimenopausal period, and the period immediately following delivery of a baby.

After giving birth, women may feel a range of emotions from numbness and sadness to irritability, confusion, and anxiety. These feelings may be an indication of depression in one of three different intensities: the baby blues, serious psychosis, and depression. The baby blues is very common, while the other two are relatively rare.

The Baby Blues. This has also been referred to as *postpartum blues* or *maternity blues.* This is the mildest and most common experience for new mothers. It often gets the entire family's attention because mom's mood shifts suddenly. She becomes irritable, she worries more, cries more, and sleeps less. When she should be caring for herself the most, she eats too much or doesn't eat enough. Everyone is surprised when she is sad within a week of becoming a mother because they thought the new baby would bring inextinguishable joy to Mom's heart. Just about the time action seems warranted, the symptoms rapidly disappear and life returns to normal. The best thing family members and friends can do is to be available and supportive.

Postnatal Psychosis. This is the truly devastating depression that is very rare but must be taken seriously if it appears. It is also referred to as *puerperal psychosis* and *postpartum psychosis.* Symptoms can include manic episodes where mom feels she is invincible. She will feel capable of anything and will adamantly argue with anyone who thinks she isn't. She may claim that she never had a baby at all. Or she may think she has given birth to an offspring of God or even the devil himself. These manic episodes can be so vivid that they prohibit reasoning with the new mother and convincing her that her perspective is way off. On the other end of the spectrum, some new moms experience deep depression that makes the responsibilities of life overwhelming and confusing to her. For the unfortunate few who will experience this, symptoms will appear somewhere between one and three months after the baby is born. This is a very serious condition and will generally result in mom being a danger to herself and others. Immediate medical attention is required.

Postnatal Depression. Between the two extremes of the relatively mild postnatal blues and the extreme postpartum psychosis is a unique and serious condition called *postnatal depression,* also commonly referred to as *postpartum depression* (PPD). This is similar to postnatal blues, but it is more intense and lasts longer. Less than one-fourth of new moms will experience this level of depression, but the illness can last six months or more. Mom will be very lethargic and despondent. She will cry often, and even though she talks about her sadness, she wakes up the next morning with the same black cloud hanging over her head. She will most likely feel like a failure as a mom and a wife since the most menial tasks are difficult for her to complete. She is not necessarily a danger to anyone, but she is living far below her potential.

Although childbirth is one of the great milestones of life, it is increasingly being recognized as one of the major physical, psychological, and social stress inducers for women. One way to differentiate between temporary baby blues and the more serious postpartum depression (PPD) is to be informed of the symptoms. Liz Mills has compiled a helpful survey you can take to determine whether you are experiencing mild symptoms or you should seek out professional help. The survey is called the *Mills Depression & Anxiety Symptom-Feeling Checklist* and can be found on the Web at www.pndsa.co.za/ms-fc.htm. We encourage you to take time to visit this site and work through the checklist. Even if you have no signs of depression, it is a good resource for you to be familiar with so you can recommend it to friends who may benefit from it.

Whether you are in the postpartum stage of life or not, one clear fact from this test that applies to all stages of change in a woman's life is this: If you are so sad that you are thinking the answer to the change is to harm yourself or harm another, then you need to seek immediate professional help. You don't have to handle depression alone. Help is available. Please don't wait until you are charged with child endangerment or worse. The moment you feel you are not your usual chipper, happy, contented self, call for help. Tell your husband. Tell a friend who may have experienced depression in the past. Talk to your mother, sister, or aunt. And talk to a doctor and counselor. Take the initiative the moment you feel depression is affecting your ability to function or any of your relationships.

Diagnosis: Deep Desperate Depression

Childbirth and motherhood are strenuous activities. All women experience weight and appetite changes after giving birth, and sleep deprivation is universal in early motherhood. An informed diagnosis is vital so that the normal strain of being a mom is not confused with depression. Honest discussions with your doctor and other moms who have been through the experience are invaluable. Books, magazines, and the Internet can also help you adjust to this new challenge.

We must remember that PPD can affect any new mother. However, some factors may place certain women at particular risk. Family history influences your susceptibility to PPD. If your family has experienced a pattern of depression, you should let your doctor know. If you have had a bout with depression prior to your pregnancy, you should have an honest conversation with your doctor. If you have been depressed without being pregnant, you have a greater risk of experiencing PPD. If you have had a prior episode of PPD, your susceptibility to a future episode is even greater.

In addition, women who are in marriages that are in turmoil, women who lack strong social support, women who do not have childcare support they can trust, and women in abusive relationships are at an increased risk for PPD. Conversely, women who have a generally positive attitude toward themselves and the state of their lives are less likely to experience depression in any form. On the other hand, women with a negative view of themselves and their world or with an abnormal need to control their environment are more likely to be depressed.

Why Am I Depressed?

Women have a very complicated set of hormones, and if one is out of whack, we feel out of sorts! Just as many variables can make us feel stressed, depressed, or overwhelmed, so many options are available to help us combat the feelings. Using biology to manage biology is smart. God says that we are "fearfully and wonderfully made." Our bodies respond to many cause and effect principles.

Consider our hormones as an environment. The earth is an environment, and when people litter, when companies dump toxins, when we strip the land of natural resources, we miss out on much of the beauty. We may cause natural disasters, soil erosion, or the extinction of some species of wildlife. When we are good stewards of our environment, the beauty and safety return.

In the same way, when we pollute our lives with bad habits (eating the wrong foods, sleeping poorly, carrying an inappropriate amount of responsibilities), we contribute to a negative environment. However, if we treat our bodies well, we improve the environment. In a sense, we are using God's creation to strengthen God's creation. And we are the capstone of God's creation![2]

Male Melancholy

A dad can also have a major adjustment as baby makes three. He may feel he has to vie for his wife's attention. He may feel left out, ignored, and possibly even jealous. Bill likes to joke, "Pam would hear Brock cry and run to him and say, 'Oh, sweetie, honey, what can I do to help?' She'd see me cry and say, 'Get over it!' " (I [Bill] didn't really cry, but I did have to adjust to sharing Pam's affections. I soon discovered Pam's love wasn't divided. It multiplies with each person that becomes a part of our family.)

One of the best ways a woman can support this fragile male ego moment is to simply say thanks. Admire and appreciate your husband when he does anything to help. Don't expect him to drop everything, run to you, fan you, and drop grapes in your mouth. Instead, remember that many women don't even have a partner to help with the baby. Thank him for being the kind of guy who hangs in there with all your emotions, all the responsibilities, and all the changes. Just say thanks.

Girl Power

Take good care of yourself!

- Do you take time to have a leisurely bath or shower?

- Do you take time to brush your teeth? Wash your face? Change your clothes? (Are you getting out of your pajamas?)

- Do you have three distinct meals a day? Do you sit down during those meals? Do you eat without a child or baby on your lap?

- Do you accept help when help is offered? Do you ask for help when you need it?

- Do you have friends you can call when you feel down, friends who will really listen? Do you let them know you need to talk?

- Do you rest or nap while your children nap? Do you ask your husband for help at night? Many husbands bring their baby to mom to nurse at night and then take the baby back to the crib. If the baby is on a bottle, dad can take a shift.

- Do you have someone watch your children so you can go out and do something you really enjoy?

- Do you buy things for yourself and not just for the kids?

- Do you allow yourself to sit without worrying about all the work you have to do? Do you read a magazine or book just for pleasure? Watch a movie?

- Do you get enough fun exercise? Take a walk, put on an exercise video, or join a class. Even putting the baby in the stroller and going for a trek around the block can help lift spirits.

- Do you say yes or no to sex because that's what you want?

- Do you make time for solitude if you want it? Are you reading the Bible, listening to calming music or praise songs, or using other relaxation activities?

- Are you looking for ways to laugh? Smile? Enjoy a few of the things you enjoyed before the baby arrived? A ten-minute walk into a favorite store can help lift your heart.

What's a Guy to Do?

- Husbands, brothers, and fathers, listen and encourage the new mother in your life to talk about her feelings. Try to express that you care and are seeking to understand.

- Husbands, find out whom she does and doesn't want to see and talk with. Run interference for her so she can recover.

- If friends or family offer to help, give them ideas: do the dishes, grocery shop, or take older children out to play.

- Husbands, try to spend time alone with your wife. You are still a couple.

- Husbands, reassure your wife of your affection and commitment. Say "I love you" often.

- Pitch in with chores and responsibilities. You may work full-time, but she carried the baby for nine months *alone*. Express gratitude with tangible help, or hire a maid!

- Husbands, be physically affectionate without asking for sex.

- Husbands, take care of yourselves too. Lower your outside responsibilities so you can stay healthy emotionally, spiritually, and physically.

- Husbands, pray with and for her. Dads and brothers can also express care with prayers, flowers, and cards.

- Through pregnancy and postpartum months, find every way possible to celebrate anything positive you see. Create ways to celebrate the new mom.

What's Next?

Some women experience an emotional oasis. It's that time after your children are in school but not yet too far into their teens, after you have "discovered yourself" and are using your talents and God-given gifts, but before perimenopause hits and slows you down. This can be a very productive time of life. For example, my years between 1994 and 2004 have been fast-paced and exciting. I enjoyed watching my children soar and succeed. Bill and I ministered as a team and supported each other's independent projects.

But seasons change. The joy of pushing on a deadline was replaced by aches and pains the next morning. My teens' lives became more complex. I had to get bifocals and adjust to a slower reading pace. My husband's family history of high blood pressure repeated itself in him at 44, and my family's history of high cholesterol hit me about the same time. We said goodbye to our local church ministry—a heart-breaking move—in the middle of Bill's midlife transition.

Our oasis time was over. The reality of midlife had hit.

Praise God for the oasis years. Enjoy them—and make the most of them! Maximize your influence for good and for God. An elderly man who had been a famous preacher told a friend of mine, "When it's your turn at bat, swing hard...you don't know when it won't be your turn at bat anymore." Good advice.

However, the next stage of life isn't bad—just very different. It too is a time of constant change. Kids become teens and then young adults who leave home. You have graduations, weddings, and baby showers. You also have more doctors' appointments. You have tough lifestyle and career decisions as you near retirement. Your midlife emotional issues challenge your ability to handle change.

What habits, principles, and character qualities can you establish now that will prepare you for this lifestage of perpetual change?

Navigating Change

A few principles that served me well as a young woman still guide me as I scan the horizon of the second half of life with its changing landscape. The principles are timeless, so they can help you navigate change whether you are 16, 46, or 96!

God Is Bigger

One of the wisest decisions I made was to really get to know God personally. I studied His character, His names, and how He relates to people. God became my best friend. My view of God grew. I learned that God is able to handle anything. Midlife will feel out of control without a big God. I have peace even at midlife because I know God loves me. He has a plan for me that will bring me a future and a hope. He is able to work all things together for my good. I used a daily mantra to forge forward in midlife: *Even when people aren't good, God is good. Even when circumstances aren't good, God is good. Even when I am not good, God is good.* A good God is able to ultimately work all things together for everyone's good.

Forward Focus

Midlife is full of opportunities. If you relive regret, people's ungratefulness, their lack of respect for you, or any of the other hurtful things people did to you in the past, you can become negative, bitter, and harsh—and then no one will want to be around you. If you focus forward and look to God for the next great opportunity, you will discover more opportunities than you can implement. At one very hard and hurtful juncture in my midlife years, I had to literally post hope. I made posters with the word *hope* blazoned on them. Under the word *hope* was a beautiful picture of a sunrise, and under the picture was Philippians 3:12-14:

> Not that I have already obtained all this, or have already been made perfect, but I press on to take hold of that for which Christ Jesus took hold of me. Brothers, I do not consider myself yet to have taken hold of it. But one thing I do: Forgetting what is behind and straining toward what is ahead, I press on toward the goal to win the prize for which God has called me heavenward in Christ Jesus.

For my birthday that year, I asked my friends for the "present of God's presence." I asked for a verse of hope I could post, memorize, and meditate on. Here are a few of my favorites. Perhaps one might encourage you as you embrace a change in your own life:

> Forget the former things; do not dwell in the past. See, I am doing a new thing....I am making a way in the desert and streams in the wasteland (Isaiah 43:18-19).

> Do not be afraid or discouraged....For the battle is not yours but God's....Go out to face them tomorrow, and the LORD will be with you (2 Chronicles 20:15,17).

> The eyes of the LORD are on those who fear Him, on those whose hope is in His unfailing love....He is our help and shield....May your unfailing love rest upon us...even as we put our hope in you (Psalm 33:18,20,22).

I was amazed to see how positive my mood became when I chose a forward focus. By improving my attitude, I partnered with God, and the changes in my life moved me forward emotionally, financially, physically, socially, and spiritually. But choosing a forward focus is not easy, nor is it a onetime thing. It's a daily practice, a carefully practiced discipline with a great payoff. You can't change circumstances, and you can't change people, but one thing you can change is your attitude. I appreciate our friends, Dave and Claudia Arp, authors of *The Second Half of Marriage*, who say, "The rest is the best." The second half of life can be full and rich because you have gained perspective, wisdom, and the ability to maximize your talents, gifts, and dreams for the greatest positive impact. Midlife is when you and your generation are in charge. With a forward focus, you can implement change for the better.

Practice Praise

The Bible says we are to give thanks in all things (1 Thessalonians 5:18), we are to give a sacrifice of praise (Hebrews 13:15), and we are to present our requests to God with praise (Philippians 4:6). The result in our life will be peace that surpasses all understanding (Philippians 4:7). And the one thing you need at midlife is personal peace. Here are a few more habits I developed as a college student that are still paying off in big ways in midlife.

Hunt for God. Each day I look for the positive thing, person, or principle God will bring across my path. By looking for God working in my life, I gain hope and peace. I never feel abandoned or sidelined, because God is at work.

Praise first. Praising God in prayer is the way I like to start my day. A morning walk, when I thank God for creation, for people, for opportunities, and even for obstacles, gives each day a fresh start. Change is easier to navigate in bite-sized pieces. Practicing praise helps you do that.

Praising first works in relationships too. Focus on and compliment the positive in people. Even the most negative and hard to love people are easier to tolerate when you love them by faith.

Bill Bright's little Transferable Concepts book *How to Love by Faith* taught me to love someone not because they were lovely but simply because God loved them. I learned how to be a conduit or funnel through which God's love could flow to others. This is important at midlife because relationships change so much. You transition from being your children's parent to being their friend and confidant. Your marriage changes as children leave the nest. What was once a cute quirk in a spouse can become a huge source of irritation if you forget to love by faith. And at midlife, you have been around the block enough times to know people who have hurt you, betrayed you, and even rejected or abandoned you. Only loving by faith and practicing praise will keep you from becoming negative, cynical, and bitter. Praise will make you better instead of bitter.

Choose joy. At one particularly tough time, I wasn't sure how to answer people when they asked, "How are you doing?" If I told them how I really felt, they could easily misunderstand. If the person listening was kindhearted and not judgmental, she or he might feel compelled to rescue me from my feelings (a job that really only God could do). So I decided to answer according to what I was choosing to do. I was making choices I knew would eventually get me to a solid emotional place again. I was choosing joy. So when people asked, "How are you, Pam?" I'd answer, "I'm choosing joy."

Howard Hendrix, professor and chairman of the Center for Christian Leadership at Dallas Theological Seminary, often wondered why people would say they were "pretty good under the circumstances." He'd reply, "What are you doing under there?" The only way to get out from under life's circumstances is to choose joy. Joy is a decision, not just a feeling.

The Bible says, "A cheerful heart is good medicine" (Proverbs 17:22). Bill and I have always valued a good laugh as a healing agent. We e-mail jokes back and forth, slide funny cards under each other's doors at work, buy calendars with funny cartoons, and share humorous stories while passing in the hallway. If I am feeling like I am going to die, then I am going to die laughing!

One day a friend e-mailed me an essay that won the 2003 Erma Bombeck Award for Humor Writing.

The First Time's Always the Worst

The first mammogram is the worst. Especially when the machine catches on fire.

That's what happened to me. The technician, Gail, positioned me exactly as she wanted me (think a really complicated game of Twister—right hand on the blue, left shoulder on the yellow, right breast as far away as humanly possible from the rest of your body). Then she clamped the machine down so tight, I think my breast actually turned inside out. I'm pretty sure Victoria's Secret doesn't have a bra for that.

Suddenly, there was a loud popping noise. I looked down at my right breast to make sure it hadn't exploded. Nope, it was still flat as a pancake and still attached to my body.

"Oh no!" Gail said loudly. These are perhaps, the words you least want to hear from any health professional. Suddenly, she came flying past me, her lab coat whipping behind her, on her way out the door. She yelled over her shoulder, "The machine's on fire, I'm going to get help!"

OK, I was wrong, "The machine's on fire" are the worst words you can hear from a health professional. Especially if you're all alone and semi-permanently attached to A MACHINE and don't know if it's THE MACHINE in question.

I struggled for a few seconds, trying to get free, but even Houdini couldn't have escaped. I decided to go to plan B: yelling at the top of my lung (the one that was still working).

I hadn't seen anything on fire, so my panic hadn't quite reached epic proportions. But then I started to smell smoke coming from behind the partition. *This is ridiculous*, I thought.

I can't die like this. What would they put in my obituary? Cause of death: breast entrapment?

I may have inhaled some fumes because I started to hallucinate. An imaginary fireman rushed in with a firehose and a hatchet. "Howdy, ma'am," he said. "What's happened here?" he asked, averting his eyes.

"My breasts were too hot for the machine," I quipped as my imaginary fireman ran out of the room again. "This is gonna take the Jaws of Life!" In reality, Gail returned with a fire extinguisher and put out the fire.

She gave me a big smile and released me from the machine. "Sorry! That's the first time that's ever happened. Why don't you take a few minutes to relax before we finish up?"

I think that's what she said. I was running across the parking lot in my backless paper gown at the time. After I'd relaxed for a few years, I figured I might go back. But I was bringing my own fire extinguisher.[4]

Embrace change by cultivating a big view of God. Go after great information on the changes you face, practice praise, and choose joy. You can harness your hormones and focus on gaining the lifestyle you desire. One of my favorite quotes on change is from George Eliot: "It is never too late to be what you might have been." Whom do you want to be?

One change that women dread is the need for a yearly mammogram. Here are some ways to prepare for a mammogram:

A mammogram is an x-ray that has its own name because no one wants to actually say the word *breast*. Mammograms require your breast to do gymnastics. If you have extremely agile breasts, you should do fine. Most breasts, however, pretty much hang around doing nothing in particular, so they are woefully unprepared. But you can prepare for a mammogram right at home using these simple exercises!

Exercise 1:

Open your refrigerator door and insert one breast between the door and the main box. Have one of your strongest friends slam the door shut as hard as possible and lean on the door for good measure. Hold that position for five seconds. Repeat.

Exercise 2:

Visit your garage at three A.M. when the temperature of the cement floor is just perfect. Take off all your clothes and lie comfortably on the floor with one breast wedged under the rear tire of the car. Ask a friend to slowly back the car up until your breast is sufficiently flattened and chilled. Turn over and repeat for the other breast.

Exercise 3:

Freeze two metal bookends overnight. Strip to the waist. Invite a stranger to squish one of your breasts between the two bookends, smashing the bookends together as hard as possible. Set an appointment with the stranger to meet next year and do it again.

Exercise 4:

Locate a pasta maker or old wringer washer. Feed the breast into the machine and start cranking. Repeat twice daily.

Why Did You Do That?

1. What major life changes have you already experienced?

2. What changes are still ahead?

3. How do you think your relationships have weathered change thus far?

4. What did you learn that can help you navigate change in the future?

5. If so much of a woman's life is change, how should business, education, media, and other institutions in society respond?

6. What are your feelings about the "mommy track" or the belief that corporations should make accommodations for pregnancy and family issues? Do you think those accommodations should be for women only or for both genders?

7. What information in this chapter should people learn early in life?

You must do the things you think you cannot do.
—ELEANOR ROOSEVELT

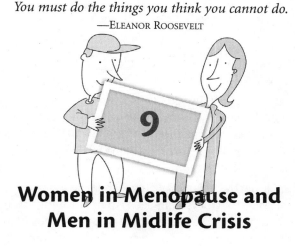

Women in Menopause and Men in Midlife Crisis

Jeff was a very conservative pastor. Each Sunday, he preached in a blue blazer, khaki pants, and a coordinating tie. Then he hit midlife. One day he appeared in a Hawaiian shirt buttoned halfway up, shorts, and Birkenstocks. He grew his hair out until it reached his shoulders. He pierced his ear and threatened to get a tattoo. Jeff and his wife Karen had eight children but he talked about selling the family van to get a Harley. He listened to his favorite rock tunes from high school, like "Born to Be Wild." Karen said to me, "Who stole my husband, and when will they bring him back?"

Men and midlife. They have some telltale signs: They trade in the practical sedan for a new sports car, trade in responsibilities for new toys like a boat, hang glider, or airplane, and all too often they trade in the wife—who has helped him build his business, his family, and a life—for a younger trophy wife. Arm candy.

Meanwhile, Mom has her own issues. Recently, a friend and I were chatting about the changes menopause brings. The hot flashes and

167

the weight gain weren't as disturbing as the signs that we were losing our minds.

> "Do you have trouble focusing when someone is talking to you?"
>
> "Yes! And even though I am listening, I can't repeat what was said! I used to be able to, word for word!"
>
> "And the emotions! I feel like I am fighting depression. I am not a negative person. This is a new thing to deal with."

How can a marriage hang together when each person is in crisis? How can marriage partners help each other through this important stage of life? If they handle the midlife issues well, they gain a deeper understanding, appreciation, and respect for each other. If they turn inward, away from each other, they create distance and walls. Midlife for men and menopause for women can be emotionally painful times. The easy way out is to run from the pain. Some midlifers blame their spouses for their own pain. They run to the new and novel to try to ease the emotional pain. However, if you run away from life, marriage, or family, you take your pain and baggage with you into a new relationship. One midlife man who left his family for another woman said, "I thought running away from the stress, the frustration, and the issues confronting me would help me find myself again. The problem is that I *did* find myself. I found I was just as big a mess, but now I had two families to support and kids that hated me, compounding the initial pain. I went to find myself, and I found out no matter how far and how fast I ran, when I arrived I was still there! I still had all the pain. I'd just taken it on a road trip."

Ladies First

In the last chapter, we looked at skills that can help us navigate change. With these in place, let's look at the ultimate change in a woman's life: menopause. Thousands of women are entering menopause in the United States every day. Perimenopause is the two-to-fifteen year span prior to menopause. For some women the perimenopause period may be short—only a year or two. For others it may be as long as seven to ten years or even more. Some women in their late thirties and early forties may begin to show symptoms. The majority of women will begin to notice symptoms between 40 and 50.

The average age for American women to enter menopause is 51. However, it can occur between a woman's late thirties and her late fifties. The term *menopause* comes from two Greek words that mean "month" and "to end." Menopause is the absence of menstruation for 12 months. Menopause also occurs when a woman's uterus and ovaries are surgically removed.

When a woman is approaching the end of her monthly cycles, she begins to experience an imbalance in her hormones, prompting complaints of increased fatigue, unexplained weight gain, breast tenderness, night sweats, insomnia, and worsening PMS. Correcting this imbalance early helps ensure a better quality of life later. Hormonal imbalance can be the result of insufficient progesterone production due to lack of regular ovulation, resulting in estrogen excess. Perimenopause is the time before menopause when levels of estrogen and progesterone decline. For some women, perimenopause can be worse than actual menopause itself.

Signs and Symptoms of Perimenopause and Menopause

During true menopause, estrogen and progesterone levels are low and fairly constant. However, during perimenopause, hormone levels may fluctuate in an irregular pattern. Some perimenopausal women have an exacerbation of their premenstrual symptoms. Signs of perimenopause include...

- *Hot flashes* or power surges—The sense of warmth starts suddenly, usually over your face, neck, and chest. Hot flashes are experienced by up to two-thirds of perimenopausal women. Hot flashes usually occur one to five years before the end of menstruation. These symptoms are more severe in women who have had their ovaries surgically removed. Hormonal changes trick the body into thinking it is too hot. To cool itself, blood is rushed to the surface of the skin, resulting in a flushed appearance. This may be the cause of the hot flash. A woman suddenly feels hot and may perspire profusely. She may then have a cold chill. Hot flashes are more common at night but can occur at any time of day. They last from a few seconds up to an hour.

- *Night sweats*—Hot flashes can interfere with sleep.

- *Cold flashes*—Make you feel clammy.

- *Vaginal dryness,* itching, and irritation—Lowered estrogen levels cause the lining of the vagina to become drier and thinner. This may lead to painful intercourse and decreased interest in sexual relations.

- *Urinary tract infections*—need to urinate frequently, burning on urination, itching in the urethra area.

- *Urinary incontinence,* especially upon sneezing and laughing—the uterus and bladder slip lower into the pelvis. Urinary leakage may be related to pelvic floor changes that occurred years ago during labor and delivery. As the estrogen level drops, further changes can occur. Low estrogen levels may weaken the urethral sphincter that helps hold in urine. If the woman has gained weight, she may have more strain on the bladder.

- *Osteoporosis* or bone density loss occurs when estrogen diminishes to a low level. The most rapid bone loss occurs during the first ten years of menopause.

- *Heart rate rises* after menopause. Estrogen helped to dilate the arteries. Menopausal women are at greater risk of heart attacks.

- *Skin changes* and increase in wrinkles—Decreasing estrogen levels make the skin less elastic.

- *Mood changes and irritability*—Mood swings, sudden tears, and even rage may be more common, and more likely in women who have had difficulty with PMS. Estrogen levels may influence the production of serotonin. Serotonin is the hormone that makes women feel happy. Lowered levels lead to depression and other negative emotions.

- *Insomnia* or other trouble sleeping is a common complaint of women in perimenopause or menopause itself. Night sweats may disrupt sleep. Irritability and depression can impair sleep.

- *Irregular periods*—Periods may become shorter or longer, lighter or heavier. Phantom periods may occur. Cramping may increase or decrease. Eventually, menses lighten, become less frequent, and then stop.

- *Change in libido* (decrease or increase). A significant number of women report a decrease in sexual desire after the age of fifty. This is matched, however, by an equal number of women who report improved sexual desire. Competing influences in a woman's life vie for her sexual interest. Lower levels of estrogen and constant change in the way her body functions draws her interest down. At the same time, more time with her husband, a greater level of privacy, the absence of any worry of getting pregnant, and the increased maturity in her own spirit makes sexual activity more appealing.

- *Fatigue*

- *Feelings of dread and anxiety,* feeling ill at ease, apprehension, doom (includes thoughts of death, picturing one's own death)

- *Difficulty concentrating,* disorientation, and mental confusion—Some women experience difficulty with memory, attention span, concentration or remembering specific words. A woman with attention deficit disorder may first come for treatment at this age because declining estrogen levels have exacerbated her ability to concentrate.

- *Itchy, crawly skin*—The skin can feel as if ants were crawling under it.

- *Aching*—sore joints, muscles, and tendons

- *Breast tenderness*

- *Headache change*—They may increase or decrease.

- *Gastrointestinal distress* can include indigestion, flatulence, gas pain, nausea, and sudden bouts of bloat.

- *Depression*

- *Exacerbation of existing conditions*—Things you have already seem to get worse.

- *Increase in allergies*

- *Weight gain* around the waist and thighs—On average, women may experience a gain of approximately ten to fifteen pounds in the years surrounding menopause.

- *Hair loss* or thinning on the head or the whole body is usually temporary in women and rarely of concern. An increase in facial hair is also usually slight and controllable by tweezing.

- *Dizziness,* light-headedness, episodes of loss of balance

- *Changes in body odor*

- *Electric shock* sensation under the skin and in the head
- *Tingling in the extremities* can also be a symptom of B₁₂ deficiency or diabetes. The tingling can result from an alteration in the flexibility of blood vessels in the extremities.
- *Gum problems, increased bleeding*
- *Burning tongue*
- *Brittle fingernails* that peel and break easily

Excited? More likely, depressed, right? But at least if you know what to expect, you won't think you are going crazy or have some horrible disease if any of these things begin to happen. No, you are just becoming a wise, maturing woman.

Jill Briscoe recalls a scene at a grand opening of a new hospital. She was a guest of honor and sitting on the front row when one of the patients of the Alzheimer wing came up to her and began asking her some unusual questions. Thinking the patient might be confusing her with a member of the hospital staff, Jill said to the elderly woman, "I'm afraid I am not who you think I am. Do you know who I am?" To which the sweet woman replied, "Well…no, dear, but if you go to the front desk they will tell you."

Call it mental-pause, or a menopausal moment. Women at midlife finally have their act together—we just forgot where we put it! I do want to grow older graciously. I want to think I'd be as encouraging as this e-mail greeting my mother sent me:

> May your hair, your teeth, your face-lift, your abs, and your stocks not fall; and may your blood pressure, your triglycerides, your cholesterol, your white blood count and your mortgage interest not rise.
>
> May you get a clean bill of health from your dentist, your cardiologist, your gastroenterologist, your urologist, your proctologist, your podiatrist, your psychiatrist, your plumber, and the IRS.

May you find yourself seated around the dinner table, together with your beloved family and cherished friends.

May what you see in the mirror delight you, and what others see in you delight them.

Hot Flash!

Hot flashes are common and inconvenient companions to midlife women. Some of my friends shared the following statements:

"Right in the middle of a nice meal, I just started sweating. I asked if it was hot in the restaurant, but everyone else said it was just fine. It got so bad that I had to walk outside to cool down."

"At first, I thought I had a fever. First I was hot. Then I was cold. Then I was hot. Then I was cold. It happened on and off all day. The first bout lasted for about 15 minutes and then went away for a couple of hours. It was one of the craziest days of my life."

"I started being impossible to sleep with. I started off with a blanket, but in the middle of the night I was so hot I just threw the covers off. An hour later I was so cold I pulled them all back up. My husband can't stand it, but I cannot get comfortable."

"I hate it when it hits. Not only do I get hot; I also get dizzy. It doesn't matter if I am in the middle of a meeting or running errands. My heart just starts to race and my knees get weak. If I don't sit down, I am afraid I am going to fall down."

"I used to dress so that I would look good. Now I dress so I will feel good. I am constantly taking layers off and putting layers on. Will this ever stop?"

Hot Flash Help

- Dress in thin layers. You can peel off the top layer when a hot flash occurs (without getting arrested!). Drink a glass of cold water or juice at the onset of a flash.

- At night, keep a carafe or thermos of ice water or an ice pack alongside your bed. Many stores sell tubes of cotton material that are filled with natural substances (usually a grain). You can freeze them and place one around your neck to cool you down or on your forehead if you get a migraine. Buy several so one is always "on ice." In a pinch, a bag of frozen vegetables will do!

- Use cotton sheets, sleeping garments, lingerie, and clothing to let your skin "breathe."

- Install a ceiling fan. Or pick up some cute old-fashioned fans. Antique stores have many with darling prints. Keep them on your bedside or in your purse.

- When unanticipated hot flashes or sweats hit, especially while traveling, a handy item to have is a portable hand fan.

Self-Care During Perimenopause and Menopause

- *Revive with vitamins.* Vitamin E may alleviate hot flashes. Prevent osteoporosis by taking calcium supplements.

- *Eat foods rich in natural estrogens* including yams, lentils, oat bran, tofu, and soy milk.

- *Get plenty of relaxation and sleep.* The brain regulates its biochemistry during sleep.

- *Take time for yourself.* Read, keep a journal, or take a class you have always wanted.

- *Baby your body.* As you are aging, your skin, hair, and nails are likely to become drier and more brittle and lose their natural oils. Moisturize your skin and deep-condition your hair.

- *Exercise regularly.* This will reduce your stress and help you regulate your sleep cycle. Exercise is also one of the most effective measures in lowering cholesterol. A few minutes of exercise can stop a panic attack dead in its tracks, reduce anxiety, and lift the blues. One of the best exercises is walking—even just 20 minutes a day.

· *Become more aware of nutrition.* Think about the types of oils you use in cooking and the way you prepare your foods. Canola, sunflower, safflower, and olive oils are the best. Sunflower oil actually serves as a cleanser of your arteries to remove plaque and prevent more plaque from forming. Certain fats are good for your body. Others are bad.

· *Avoid processed foods, nicotine, caffeine, artificial sweeteners, and junk food.* These are no-no's for menopausal women. Try to cut down, or better yet, stop drinking carbonated drinks. The carbonation can cause bloating.

· *Eat as much garlic as possible.* It's excellent for blood pressure and cholesterol.

· *Eat lots of broccoli.* It's loaded with phytochemicals and vitamins, and it contains the highest amount of antioxidants of any other vegetable. Stacked with protective compounds, such as isothiocyanates and sulforaphane, as well as indole-3-carbinol (I3C), a substance that is said to have anticancer actions, broccoli tops the list of must serves. The entire brassica genus of vegetables (which includes Brussels sprouts, cauliflower, cabbage, Chinese cabbage, bok choy, kale, and collard greens), contains a compound that activates certain enzymes in the human body to protect cells from genetic damage.

· *Eat fiber-rich foods.* When our estrogen dips, our cholesterol levels often are elevated. Eat lots of fruit and fiber.

· *Avoid fried, rich, or spicy foods and too much sugar.* There's a natural craving for sweets during menopause, especially chocolate. Women at midlife are more likely to develop gallstones, so avoid spicy and fatty foods and remember that hormone replacement therapy can cause or aggravate gallbladder problems.

- *Cravings for chocolate.* Chocolate is the "feel good" food—probably raising serotonin levels. However, while it may make us feel good for a short while, it and all sweets can bring on hot flashes, raise insulin levels, and cause palpitations, anxiety, and even depression. So while everyone's exalting chocolate, remember, it's not good for every perimenopausal woman.

- *Alcoholic beverages* can also contribute to hot flashes and palpitations. They raise your triglycerides as alcohol is converted to sugar in the body. Sugar and alcohol are two of the worst offenders during perimenopause, and elevated triglycerides is one of the greatest contributors to heart disease.

- *High carbohydrate foods* can also cause hot flashes, palpitations, anxiety, and depression. They can elevate insulin levels, which can exacerbate menopausal symptoms. Too many carbohydrates can cause weight gain.

- *For the nausea* often associated with perimenopause and PMS, try a cup of boiling water with two to three teaspoons of concentrated lemon juice. Sip it slowly, and it should work like a charm every time.

- *Decide how you will handle weight gain.* You may decide that you are content with a little more weight. Your body naturally takes on weight during midlife as a way of producing more estrogen. Or you may decide that a regimen of careful diet planning and exercise are in order. Aerobic exercise will burn fat, and weight training can build muscle, which in turn burns more calories. Before you begin a new exercise routine, however, talk things through with your physician to ensure success.

- *If you drink alcoholic beverages, do so in moderation. If you smoke, stop.*

- *Learn to p-a-m-p-e-r yourself!* Hey, superwoman! Take time for yourself. You'll be amazed at how well everyone manages to get along without your constant attention. Take time to regroup. Make a quiet time for yourself. Go for a walk. Meditate on God's Word. Listen to some relaxing music or sit and dangle your feet in a cool stream. Find the few things you enjoy that bring peace and solace to your heart, and then put them into your schedule on a regular basis.

Menopause and Hormone Replacement

Perimenopausal signs and symptoms afflict up to 85 percent of all menopausal women.

Testing by an endocrinology professor at University of British Columbia discovered that 50% of all women in North America are severely deficient in progesterone by age 35; progesterone levels decrease even more during the menopausal years to almost zero; estrogen levels also decrease by some 40 to 60 percent. Progesterone deficiency increases the risks for cancer, & low progesterone levels can be the cause of irritability, anger, fits of crying and generally unstable emotions & behavior. The imbalance between estrogen & progesterone levels results in "estrogen dominance," a term describing what happens when the normal ratio or balance of estrogen to progesterone is changed....Estrogen dominance is a known cause &/or contributor to cancers, including those of the breast, ovaries, uterus, and prostate.[1]

Women suffering from estrogen dominance symptoms can still be lacking in estrogen, but they also lack progesterone. To decide how best to proceed, each woman needs to consider her own unique circumstances:

- her symptoms and their severity
- her health history and her family's health history
- her personal preferences about taking natural remedies or prescription medications

Estrogen seems to relieve many of the perimenopausal signs and symptoms. If a woman has had her uterus removed, she may consider taking estrogen alone. A doctor will probably prescribe estrogen without progesterone for a woman with an intact uterus. This choice, however, increases the risk of uterine cancer. Effective Hormone Replacement Therapy (HRT), often necessitates a combination of estrogen and progesterone.

> Women who have had endometrial cancer, breast cancer, blood clots, stroke, unexplained vaginal bleeding or liver disease should not use HRT. Likewise, if you bleed after you've ceased to have periods for several months, or if you notice any breast lumps or pain, or have any questions—call your doctor. Additionally, there are quite a few alternate or natural remedies that can provide you with options to consider.[2]

Hormone replacement therapy should only be considered after investigating all the factors in your personal situation. You should research your own psychological history, the physical risks you are most susceptible to, your personal history, and your family history. Personal research, discussion with friends, and a medical consultation are all in order if you are considering this step.

Our questions and issues change as we draw near to menopause. Women over 50 are asking, *What will keep me free of heart disease, osteoporosis, cancer, and other ailments?* Progesterone, estrogen, DHEA, pregnenolone and testosterone all become integral parts of our vocabulary and are important in maintaining a healthy balance.

After menopause, bones lose significant amounts of calcium. In 25 percent of women, this bone loss can result in osteoporosis with the resultant high risk of broken bones. Taking estrogen stops the loss of any more calcium but does not replace the calcium already lost. Taking calcium supplements and vitamin D will not replace the lost calcium either. An estrogen-androgen combination may promote new bone formation. The biggest decision most postmenopausal women will make is if and when to do HRT. For a detailed discussion of treatment options, check out the website www.nih.gov/news/NIH-Record/03_24_98/story02.htm.*

Men in Midlife

While women are passing through the changes associated with menopause, midlife men are also undergoing changes. At midlife, men come face-to-face with their own mortality. Some want to volunteer with the youth group so they can hang out and feel young again. Others buy sports cars, motorcycles, or boats, or take up new activities, such as parasailing. Others quit their jobs, feeling stuck in life. Others return to college to earn a higher degree. A few leave their marriages, find younger women, and add a whole new host of problems and issues to their midlife passage. Midlife raises the same questions in a man's heart as in a woman's, but the answers can be vastly different. Some

---

* For more information on menopause and perimenopause see the following websites:
  - "Menopause Mailing List." (www.howdyneighbor.com/menopaus/women.htm)
  - "Menopause & Peri-Menopause." (www.bcrmh.com/disorders/menopause.htm)
  - www.power-surge.com
  - www.health-science.com
  - www.buzzle.com

make wise, healthy, future-building decisions. Others take a shortcut out of their pain and seek quick solutions to in-depth issues. Sadly, many of those quick solutions can destroy a life and family.

When men hit a midlife transition, they ask a few key questions:

- Is this the career I want to continue in for the rest of my life?

- Have I made my mark on the world?

- I am mortal, and I don't like it. How can I feel young again?

- Why do I feel so lost? (He may have unresolved emotional baggage from his childhood.)

- I have spent so much time on work, I feel like a stranger in my own family. How can I get closer to my wife and children?

- I want a deep relationship. Who will listen to my heart? (The wise wife will want this to be her. The wise midlife man will seek ways to get reconnected to his wife.)

A quick perusal of these questions shows that a man must invest some emotional energy and significant time to resolve the issues on his heart. Sally Conway, a specialist in the area of midlife, gave one of my dear friends some great advice in dealing with her midlife husband. "Look at him through the eyes of an 18- or 19-year-old. What traits or qualities would an 18- or 19-year-old woman find attractive in your husband? You find them attractive too. Your spouse doesn't need another mother. Right now he needs you to be his girlfriend."

It will take time to be your husband's girlfriend. He'll need time for you to listen to his heart, to be his sounding board, to be his date and his sexual playmate. Remember Jeff and Karen, the couple at the beginning of the chapter? Karen said to me over lunch, "Pam, it takes a lot of time to be my husband's girlfriend. I have to shave my legs every day!"

Being a girlfriend to your spouse may be one of your toughest assignments. A man can feel insecure or like a failure at this stage of life. He will look to you to bolster him, but you might also be feeling a bit insecure about yourself. You might be insecure about your body's changes or your career gains or lack of them. You might be juggling the needs of teens or young adults leaving the nest. Perhaps you are caring for aging parents as well.

Karen dug in and learned as much as she could about men and midlife. She read books, went to seminars, and found a counselor specializing in midlife issues. She set aside some of her dreams, plans, and responsibilities to be his confidant and lover. She invested in things that made him feel valued: golf dates each week with him, and a recliner with built-in massage. And she encouraged him to get that Harley. (Karen said, "It is cheaper than a divorce and less complicated than if he got a girlfriend! He needs a new adventure—and he has even talked about getting me to go with him on a trip. Midlife isn't all bad!") Jeff decided to keep the family van, he cut his hair, he put back on the blue blazer (at least for Sundays), and he returned to finish his doctorate. And Jeff and Karen took a second honeymoon—part of the time on the Harley and part on a cruise.

One day Jeff said to Karen, "Honey, I've noticed how much you have set aside for me. I appreciate all the time you have listened, all the sacrifices you have made. I want to do something for you. I know you have wanted to start a national organization to equip leaders. I want to help you. Whatever I can do, just name it." Jeff is now one of Karen's best cheerleaders on a new adventure in life.

You Have to Have Friends!

One of the best decisions I made as I entered the empty nest and perimenopause was to start a support group. When my first son went off to college, I found myself with some mixed emotions. I was so proud of him. He is a leader, making a positive difference in a very negative world. But I missed him. I recognized the signs of the blues and set about finding a way to make music out of them. So I sent an invitation to everyone I knew who had at least one child out of the house, and 15 women responded. We meet once a month, and we started by discussing a chapter from the book, *I'm Too Young to Be*

This Old by Poppy Smith. What I thought was going to be a simple, temporary book study is turning into a friendship circle that keeps all of our heads above water!

I have found such comfort and hope in having a group of friends who simply understand. I don't have to explain anything because they know what I'm talking about. They too are struggling to stay in shape. They too are facing down demons of fear for their children, their health, or their aging parent.

Our monthly meetings are the antithesis of PMS. They are Positive Moms Standing because we are standing together. We pray for one another, enjoy each other's company and struggles, and offer a strong shoulder (or a flabby forearm) to lean on.

A few of my mentors set the example for me. They are a group of friends who all served in Bible Study Fellowship together, raised their kids together, and now are facing midlife years together. They call themselves the Lunch Bunch. They simply go out for a nice leisurely lunch once a month, exchange prayer requests, and laugh a lot. Another group of friends over 50 decided they would take an outdoor adventure each year to keep themselves challenged and depending on God. They wanted to keep growing and stretching, and they discovered that a group of women backpacking or whitewater rafting definitely did the trick. After each adventure, the women feel more competent and capable to handle whatever life throws at them. Another group has a girlfriends' getaway each year where they come, scrapbook, share secrets of the heart and soul, and do something outrageously fun like karaoke or line dancing.

Finishing Well

I think the leader on the cutting edge of "meno mama" is Barbara Johnson. Her book *Hanging Between Menopause and Death* was packed with second-half-of-life humor, and women flocked to Women of Faith conferences to hear her speak. Her decision to have joy regardless of what life threw her way was and is a rally cry for squeezing the most out of the last years of life. In the past year, Barbara has stepped off the Women of Faith tour to battle a war against cancer. I don't know how the war against this dreaded disease will end for her, but I do know without a shadow of a doubt Barbara will finish the race well.

That's how I want to finish—well. Jill Briscoe and I had lunch while she was writing her book *Finishing Well*. I didn't need to wait until the book was published to learn how to finish well—she was modeling it! While other women retire, move to Florida, and play cards, Jill travels around the globe with her husband or sometimes alone, bringing encouragement and equipping to women worldwide. She has found a great adventure.

One of the main transitions that often coincides with either perimenopause or menopause is the empty nest. At this stage of life, a woman is in a defining point, much like the evaluation that she had in her early twenties or thirties when she asked, *Who am I, God?* At this crossroads, as her children leave home and she finds she has expendable time, she asks, *With the remaining years, what can I do that will really matter? What will leave a lasting legacy?* She goes on a search for significance.

In our support group, one of the most challenging questions we have discussed is, What have you always wanted to do but were too afraid or too busy to do until now? What is a great adventure you'd like to do before your body wears out? What is a dream yet unfulfilled? What is a goal God has yet to accomplish?

My friend Natalie and I have made a commitment that we will encourage each other to keep being positive, to keep living for good and for God regardless of how old we get. It started when I gave Natalie the poem entitled, "When I Am Old I Shall Wear Purple." Every time we wear purple, we remember to keep going, keep striving, and keep positive no matter what. Do you have a friend whom you could send a little "purple" to?

A Prayer Partner

Only another woman who has experienced midlife will really understand the unique pressure of this stage of life. This is a great time for a trusted prayer partner—someone who will share your burdens, and you hers. Having faith in God for a friend's problems is sometimes easier than trusting Him to solve your own. Borrow each other's faith to make it through. Share romantic ideas and cheer each other on as you seek to minister hope and help to the midlife men you are married to. Whew! With a few good friends and God, you can finish well!

Girl Power

Instead of allowing perimenopause and your hormones to totally control your life, give God the reins!

- Pray daily for God's wisdom. Ask Him to help you learn as much as you can. Find the best experts to help you.

- Pray moment by moment for the Holy Spirit's power to control you. Instead of giving in to the negative emotions, ask God for supernatural power to cope. Choose words and actions ahead of time. Decide what kind of person you want to be, and choose actions, words, and support systems that will help you achieve the positive results you want.

- Protect your relationships. Don't use perimenopause for an excuse when relational stress may be caused by other factors, but on those hard-to-cope days, help those nearest you to adjust their expectations and not add to your stress.

- Persistence pays off. Don't give up. Don't give in. Keep seeking help, support groups, newsletters, counselors, doctors, books. Keep going until you find the best treatment for you. God thinks you deserve the best. After all, Jesus died on the cross for you! So, love yourself as much as God does, and seek to be the best woman you can be.

- Pamper yourself along the way. Take time to smell the roses, rest, read. Practice self-care so that you have the emotional and physical strength to give care to those you love the most.

- Prepare for midlife by learning as much as you can about how men think and feel at this stage of life. Help your spouse by encouraging him to deal with unresolved issues from childhood, and listen to his heart as he seeks to find and live out the adventure on his heart.

What's a Guy to Do?

- Team up! Any transition your wife goes through, you go through! In pregnancy and parenthood, a good man will team up to care for his wife. Perimenopause is no different. Support her efforts to get information and help. Set aside time to listen to her. Set aside money in the budget for her to buy the tools, resources, and food she needs to feel better. Counteract the feelings of guilt that often arise during this stage of life.

- Celebrate her. Compliment her character. Bolster her confidence by reliving her past achievements and giving her words of affirmation as she steps out in new or challenging areas.

- Don't try to bolster your own self-esteem by finding "arm candy" or a "trophy wife." If your heart is wandering, get counseling. Don't traumatize your wife, your family, and your own life just because your wife is looking a little older. Take a look in the mirror. You are looking older too!

- If your wife is acting very uncharacteristically, intervene. Hormones can dramatically impact behavior. Instead of getting angry, get to the bottom of the issue. Ask your wife to get a full medical checkup. Go with her to a medical facility that specializes in menopausal issues. If she is in denial, make an appointment with a counselor, pastor, or trusted family friend to discuss the best way to intervene and explain to your wife that she deserves treatment.

Signs That You Might Be Experiencing Menopause

- You sell your home heating system at a yard sale. (Hot flashes.)

- Your husband complains about snow piling up on the bed. (Nightsweats.)

- Your husband jokes that instead of buying a wood stove, he is using you to heat the family room this winter. Rather than just saying you are not amused, you shoot him. (Mood swing.)

- You write your kids' names on Post-it notes. (Memory loss.)

- Your husband chirps, "Hi, honey, I'm home," and you reply, "Well, if it isn't Ozzie, 'he never takes out the trash or calls when he is going to be late,' Nelson." (Irritability.)

- The Phenobarbital dose that wiped out the Heaven's Gate Cult gives you four hours of decent rest. (Sleeplessness.)

- You find guacamole in your hair after a Mexican dinner. (Fatigue.)

- You change your underwear after every sneeze. (Mild incontinence.)

- You need Jaws of Life to help you out of your car after returning home from an Italian restaurant. (Sudden weight gain.)

- You ask Jiffy Lube to put you up on a hoist. (Dryness.)

- You take a sudden interest in WrestleMania. (Female hormone deficiency.)

- You're on so much estrogen that your husband of 35 years who has a receding hairline, and an extending beltline, and is standing in his ripped undershirt with a wrench in his hand, looks sexier than Brad Pitt, Mel Gibson, and Ricky Martin all rolled into one! (Hormone therapy.)

Why Did You Do That?

1. How do you feel about the transitions both men and women traverse between the ages of 35 and 55?

2. What did you learn that can help you better understand your spouse?

3. What did you learn that can help you encourage your spouse?

4. What practical change do you want to make that you believe will strengthen your relationships?

5. How could the information in this chapter impact those who make leadership decisions for institutions such as education, church, business, and government?

6. How does the information in this chapter relate to the workplace?

7. What can you do to help a friend who is either a man in midlife or a woman in menopause?

8. How can you develop friendships early in life that can help you when you hit midlife?

To avoid criticism, do nothing, say nothing, and be nothing.
—Elbert Hubbard

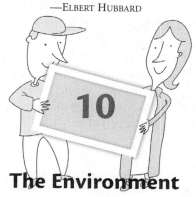

The Environment

We make our choices and our choices make us. The argument is almost as old as time: Are we predestined to act the way we do, or do we have a free will? Do we have any say in how our life turns out? Few would argue that our environment plays a significant role in our development.

Our environment includes many components, including politics, friendships, the media, family and parenting, education, religion, culture, and traumatic experiences. All those influences present us with choices, and our choices combine with our biology to form our personalities. From early childhood, we have been making choices that deeply impact our life and our thinking. In this chapter, we will explore a few more elements of our environment as well as some tools to help you better understand yourself, your spouse, and your family. These considerations may also help you improve your work and social relationships.

We encourage people to be deliberate about their choices. You can't choose your eye color, height, gender, or parents, but you *can* choose a myriad of things. Or you can choose not to choose. Those who make deliberate choices contribute to the outcome of their future.

You can choose to succeed in life regardless of what life has handed you! This chapter will give you many opportunities to have deliberate dialogue with those you love and with God. Those conversations can help you expose the deliberate choices you have made, and they can inspire you to be even more deliberate in your future choices, empowering you to actually reach your God-given potential and achieve your hopes, dreams, and goals.

Communication

One way to make good choices in your relationships is to be understanding of the people around you. People have reasons for the way they act. If you consider all that another person may be experiencing and feeling, you will be more likely to make wise choices in your relationships. How can you become more understanding of another person's situation and motivation? Let's make it simple: Stop, look, and listen.

Stop!

Avoid looking at everyone from your point of view. We were reminded of this when we were seminary students and we gathered with three other couples for a fun evening. We met at the home of our friends Mesghina and Semret. They had been married almost 15 years, and had just immigrated from Africa, escaping the brutal communist regime that had tried to kill them for their faith in God. We wanted the couples to get to know one another better, so after an amazing dinner of African food, we sat down to play Ungame. In Ungame, everyone wins because the point is to answer questions so people can become better acquainted. We had even sent for new cards specifically for this party—cards just for married couples.

Each of us took a turn reading a card and answering the question. When Mesghina drew a card he read it silently and put it down. "I cannot answer the question," he told us.

Thinking his limited English might be the problem, I picked up the card and read it aloud, and another person rephrased it. "Yes, I know what the card says," he acknowledged, "but I cannot answer that question. It is not the African way. The question is too personal." So we suggested he read a different card. He read it silently and said, "Not the African way," and put it down. I picked up a third card and said, "Maybe this one?" and read the question. Mesghina shook his head no, and we all said, "Not the African way." Finally, I said, "Forget about the game. Let's just tell about our favorite day when we were growing up." Our culture, our socioeconomic class, and our political and religious bias can all color our view of life and people. To truly tap into another person's feelings, you have to be willing to walk in their shoes, to look at life from their frame of reference.

A friend sent us the following list that illustrates the need for men and women to look at things from one another's perspective. It is simply titled, "Words Women Use."

The words we share really matter, but we can keep a sense of humor too. Here are some of the words women use:

Fine
This is the word women use to end an argument when they feel they are right, and you need to shut up. Never use *fine* to describe how a woman looks—this will cause you to have one of those arguments.

Five minutes
This is half an hour. It is equivalent to the five minutes that your football game is going to last before you take out the trash.

Nothing
This means "something," and you should be on your toes. *Nothing* is usually used to describe the feeling a woman has of wanting to turn you inside out, upside down, and backward. *Nothing* usually signifies an argument that will last "five minutes" and end with "fine."

Go ahead (with raised eyebrows)

This is a dare—one that will result in a woman getting upset over "nothing" and will end with "fine."

Go ahead (normal eyebrows)

This means "I give up" or "Do what you want because I don't care." You will get a "raised eyebrow go ahead" in just a few minutes, followed by "nothing" and "fine." She will talk to you in about "five minutes," when she cools off.

Loud sigh

This is not actually a word but a nonverbal statement often misunderstood by men. A loud sigh means she thinks you are an idiot and wonders why she is wasting her time arguing with you over "nothing."

Soft sigh

This also is not a word but a nonverbal statement. Soft sighs mean that she is content. Your best bet is to not move or breathe, and she will stay content.

That's okay

This is one of the most dangerous statements that a woman can make to a man. *That's okay* means that she wants to think long and hard before paying you back for whatever it is that you have done. *That's okay* is often used with a raised-eyebrow *fine.*

Go ahead

At some point in the near future, you are going to be in some mighty big trouble.

Please do

This is not a statement—it is an offer. A woman is giving you the chance to come up with an excuse for doing whatever it is that you have done. You have a fair chance with the truth, so be careful and you shouldn't get a "that's okay."

Thanks

A woman is thanking you. Do not faint. Just say, "You're welcome."

Thanks a lot

This is much different from *thanks*. A woman will say "Thanks a lot" when she is really ticked off at you. It signifies that you have offended her in some callous way, and it will be followed by the loud sigh. Be careful not to ask what is wrong after the loud sigh—she will only tell you "Nothing."

Look!

Become a keen observer. The television detective Monk is a bit quirky, but he's a terrific investigator because he looks for the details. If someone really observed me at a speaking engagement, they might notice that I have a ring shaped like a heart on one pinky. If they asked about that ring, they would discover what a terrific marriage I have to a terrific man because they would hear the story of when and how Bill gave me the ring. They might also notice that my purse is over-flowing, that a fingernail may be glued back on, and that I have too many Post-its stuck in my notes and in my Bible—all signs of moving at a quick pace. They'd see a picture of my family on my book table, so they would know family is important to me.

This is why I love to go to people's homes if I am trying to get to know them better. If their books are on the shelf from tallest to small-est and their clothes are hung on color-coded hangers, I'd recruit them to oversee minute and important details. If their den or office was a bit homey and disheveled, I would know I was dealing with creative, visionary people. If they displayed family pictures going back gener-ations with their children's school photos since kindergarten on the walls and a child's drawing on the refrigerator, I would know they valued children and family. If their awards and trophies were displayed, I would sense they were competitive too.

When observing someone, remember that you are gathering facts, not assessing his or her motivation. Understanding a person's motivation requires the next step.

Listen!

To really understand someone, you need to develop a great listening ear. You cannot discern motive unless the person shares and discloses it. We need to listen more and second-guess less. Too often we ask a question and then tune the person out while we rehearse our reply! Here are some listening exercises to try to hone up that listening ear:

Active listening:

- *Repeat* back key phrases the other person is saying. Key phrases usually have a feeling word in them. ("I am *afraid* we're getting into debt." "She *upset* me." "I am *frustrated* with him.")

- *Rephrase* what has been said. ("What I hear you saying is...")

- *Regroup.* Ask for clarification. Is what you heard close to what he or she said? ("So, honey, am I in the ballpark?" or "Is this what you meant?")

- *Reconnect.* Try to relate his or her feelings to your own experience. ("Could the way you are feeling be a little like I felt when...?")

Proactive listening simply means using your body to show you are listening. Lean forward. Get closer. Make eye contact. Nod. If you act like you are listening, sometimes you actually will!

Visual listening is picturing what the person is saying in your mind's eye. Try to stay tuned-in by recreating the story on the stage of your mind.

Creative listening usually works with children, but in a heated emotion-filled discussion, it can sometimes lead to deeper understanding even with adults. I might ask, "If your emotion was an animal, what animal would you be?" "If how you are feeling was a car, what car would you be?"

One creative method that works with some adults is, "Is there a movie scene that captures what you are trying to tell me?" Sometimes a line from a book, a shared memory, or even a commercial can shed some light on what the person is trying to get across to you.

Relating feelings to a common physical experience is a simple way to describe them. For example, "Do you feel as if you just fell out of a tree and the wind is knocked out of you?" "Is the grief suffocating you like someone put a plastic bag over your head?" "Are you saying that you are feeling your space is being invaded, like when you ride on a crowded elevator?"

The remaining pages of this book are devoted to other environmental factors that impact us. They present us with choices that will help create who we are. At the end of each section are questions for discussion. Don't forget to listen!

The Parent Factor

I (Pam) rang the doorbell to Jan's house and heard her husband yell, "Woman!" followed by a string of expletives. I was embarrassed for Jan and offended for all women as I heard him order Jan to bring him everything from a beer to his paper and slippers. I was only at her home a short time, but I couldn't believe Jan would or could put up with this.

Months later, Jan and I had coffee. She opened up to me. "Pam, my husband really is a nice man underneath his gruff exterior. I'm taking that *Boundaries* Bible study you recommended. Well, I told him that I would not answer him if he called me names, degraded me, or swore at me. It made him pretty mad at first. Then last night, he brought me home a card—something he rarely does. It was an apology! He finally opened up to me. Pam, we have been married for ten years and I just found out that his mom was an overbearing, negative person that always belittled her husband. Nothing he ever did and nothing any of the boys did was ever good enough for her. My husband said when he was 18 he vowed he would never let a woman control his life again. But he told me he was afraid of losing me, so he is willing to work on getting over his baggage. Do you think Bill can squeeze some time out for him?"

Or consider Trent. He grew up with a dad who was an all-American athlete, a Rhodes scholar, and president of several clubs. He now owns a successful business. But Trent was skinny and didn't really even like sports. School came hard for him. He had to study long and hard to get Bs. He felt his father was always disappointed in him. Trent felt like a failure. Trent married a sweet, supportive, encourager. But if she ever said anything negative or critical, Trent flew into a rage. She walked on eggshells in the relationship.

Or maybe your life is like Angie's: Her dad abandoned the family for 15 years. He missed her birthdays, her first dance, her first prom, graduation—and then suddenly he showed up at her dorm room door one night. She had just started seeing a counselor because she had a history of cheating on boyfriends. Her pattern had been, "I'll leave you before you leave me." Angie had to get to the bottom of her pain from her relationship with her father if she ever hoped to have the kind of long-term, committed, happy marriage she dreamed of.

To really know someone, get to know his or her parents. See how the person interacts in the family system. Some children are favored. Some are the family scapegoat. We all have a role in the family. Even our birth order can impact us.

Dr. Kevin Leman, in *The New Birth Order Book*, gives a short quiz to help the reader get a quick grasp of birth order.

Which of the following sets of personality traits fits you best?

    A. perfectionist, reliable, conscientious, list maker, well organized, hard-driving, natural leader, critical, serious, scholarly, logical, doesn't like surprises, loves computers

B. mediator, compromising, diplomatic, avoids conflict, independent, loyal to peers, many friends, a maverick, secretive, unspoiled

C. manipulative, charming, blames others, attention seeker, tenacious, people person, natural sales person, precocious, engaging, affectionate, loves surprises

D. little adult by age seven, very thorough, deliberate, high achiever, self-motivated, fearful, cautious, voracious reader, black and white thinker, uses "very," "extremely," "exactly" a lot, can't bear to fail, has very high expectations for self, more comfortable with people who are older or younger

If you noted that the test seemed rather easy because A, B, and C listed traits of the oldest right on down to the youngest in the family, you are right. If you picked list A, it's a very good bet you are firstborn in your family. If you chose list B, chances are you are a middle child….If list C seemed to relate best to who you are, it's likely you are the baby in the family….But what about list D? It describes the only child.[1]

Here are a few questions to open up the closets of a person's life. A person's family and parental issues can explain a lot. But be careful, knowing this information makes you responsible for handling it with care. Never use the knowledge you gain in any of these exercises against someone, or they will feel the ultimate betrayal. Using someone's deepest secret or most sensitive issues against them can bring a death blow to a relationship.

- What are the best traits of your father? Your mother?
- What are their weaknesses?
- What character quality in your mother and father do you want to make sure to pass on to your own children?

- What character quality did your family value the most?

- What were your grandparents' best qualities?

- What was the best day you ever spent with your dad? With your mom?

- What was the worst day with your father? With your mother?

- Do you think your parents really understand you?

- What one word would you use to describe your relationship with your parents?

The Economic Factor

My grandmother saved everything. Every egg carton, every strawberry basket from the grocery store. She rewashed and reused bread bags. She used twist ties until they were bare wire. And I knew why. She had shared many stories of Depression-era Christmases when she was a child and the only gift in her Christmas stocking was an orange.

Or maybe you know someone like my friend Pete. (His mother calls him Pedro.) He is the son of migrant farm workers. He grew up dirt-poor. His parents made sure he received an education, and Pete made sure that education made him money. He vowed he would never be poor again. When he married Leslie, they were so happy—at least Leslie thought so until Pete began to be so angry anytime she spent any money on anything.

Conversely, Shelly grew up in a wealthy home and expected that same level of comfort when she married. But her husband, Chris, just couldn't provide like her dad. A host of relational issues cropped up. Sheila is another woman who grew up in an extremely wealthy home, but her family made its money off tobacco, and she is so racked with guilt that she lives in a modest apartment and gives most of her income away to charity. Or maybe your story is like Trina's. She was raised with little, but an invention of hers has won her a very nice salary—but she feels uncomfortable in the social settings she is often invited to.

Finances cause more arguments than just about any topic in a marriage. Here are some questions that demonstrate that the real issue isn't the money or lack of it but people's attitude about it.

- How would you describe your economic status when you were growing up: poor, middle-class, upper-middle, or rich?

- Did you always seem to have what you needed?

- How was money distributed? Did your parents hand you some money when you wanted, did you have an allowance, or did you have to earn all your own money?

- What kind of home and what kind of neighborhood did you grow up in?

- Which philosophy of finance best describes your view: Do you spend what you have or earn what you need?

- How do you use expendable income (savings, pleasure items, recreation, travel, home improvement, education, giving)?

- When you were growing up, how much money did your family spend for birthday parties, Christmas, and vacations?

- Did your parents buy you your own car at 16, or did you buy your own later?

- What was your first job?

The Social Factor

Mandy seemed to have a chip on her shoulder. She always put down men, including her partner, Jack—even in front of company. They had a very unique arrangement. They lived together for ten years, never marrying. She did her thing, he did his. They functioned like two roommates. Mandy was bold, brash, and a little belligerent at times. She called herself a free spirit, but she didn't seem very free to me. Her negativity held her in bondage, locked away from true happiness. One day, on the way to a literature class social, Mandy told me about her childhood. "My mom never married. I am not sure who my dad is. She was a flower child, and then she joined the feminist revolution. She was a leader. When I was a little girl, I kept on my nightstand a picture of her burning her bra on her college's administration steps. I went to a lot of pro-women rallies. Mom is a radical feminist. She taught me that a woman is the god of her own life. She calls the shots. Mom has a lesbian lover now. No one ever told my mom what to do, and no one will tell me how to live either."

That conversation was a far cry from my roots. I was raised on a farm in the sixties. My grandparents and parents were very conservative. They shook their heads in shock and dismay over statements on television by parents who were trying to be their children's friends, who had liberal views on their children's sex lives, abortion, and drug use. Some parents were authoritarian and strict, others were liberal with no rules. Those social forces impact the next generation.

The American Family

The Mosaic generation includes people from thirteen to thirty. Their parents had a "me first" social attitude. Many of their parents enjoyed the relative prosperity of the Reagan years. However, many more of these children moved from a four-bedroom home in the suburbs to either living with grandparents or living in a tiny apartment because of divorce. They have watched their parents spend huge amounts of time at work and very little quality time at home. And those that did have time with parents might have spent most of it in the family van being shuttled from music lessons to sports to art class or other after-school activities. They are educated, enriched, and exhausted!

Consider this chart of how the time we are born impacts our attitudes:

Three Generations			
	Traditionalist born before 1946	Boomer born 1946–60	Twentysomething born 1960–80
Outlook:	practical	optimistic	skeptical
Work Ethic:	dedicated	driven	balanced
View of Authority:	respectful	love/hate	unimpressed
Leadership Style:	hierarchical	by consensus	by competence
Relationships:	self-sacrifice	gratification	reluctance to commit
Perspective:	civic-minded	team-oriented	self-reliant[2]

Geography

Geographic location can affect you as well. Those in the country and suburbs had much different childhoods from those in the city. Those in the south may have been trained in hospitality or prejudice. Those in East L.A. know street survival but feel lost in the wilderness of Montana. To know someone's childhood is to know a great deal about them.

Social Mores

Social factors like birth control, AIDS/HIV, easy access to drugs, the acceptance of drinking alcohol, and the amount of violence on TV all influence the way we think and feel. Athletes and movie stars are glorified, teachers and business owners vilified. In a strange twist of irony, the nerd you made fun of could become the next Bill Gates. Scientists and those adept at math, engineering, and computers are leading social change by opening up new options like telecommuting, instant messaging, and the Web. The social ramifications of these remain to be seen. Bill and I have seen huge interpersonal problems between people who use e-mail to try to dialogue about issues that are so emotionally charged that they should only be handled face-to-face. In person, you can read the person's body language; you can tell when you have said something that hurt them. The negative effects of distant dialogue will show up in this generation, as will the advantages of being able to stay in touch when you are halfway around the world.

Each generation has had its demons: Hitler and the Holocaust, Communist oppression, the Taliban's terrorism. Televised war and minute-to-minute terrorist updates have made the daily stress level rise. A little extra drama in a relationship can convince someone to bail more quickly than it used to. In a world where you feel you might die tomorrow, you are tempted to make choices for happiness today—for this moment—regardless of their long-term ramifications.

Youth of the past 20 years have fewer and fewer authentic positive role models. Fewer and fewer leaders are walking their talk. New lingo has formed. To be "Enroned" is to be sold out. Long-lasting, trusted friendships and marriages are difficult to maintain when the media constantly logs scenes of betrayal into your memory.

Smaller Social Circles

Our small social circles can also impact us. I have noticed that those with a large number of divorced friends are more likely to feel dissatisfied with their own marriage for little or no reason. Friendships help form us—negatively or positively. The Bible says it plainly: "Bad company corrupts good morals." You are whom you hang out with.

Here are a few questions to discern what social factors, slogans, and teaching may be influencing the people you are wanting to understand:

- What key phrases do you remember learning from teachers?

- What slogans from television commercials do you recall?

- What books have made the deepest impact on you?

- What world leaders do you respect and why?

- What fads did you conform to while growing up?

- Who were your role models as a child? As a teen? In college and young adulthood?

- What picture books did your mother or child-care worker read to you as a preschooler?

- What were the popular slogans of your generation? ("Free love," "Just say no," "A mind is a terrible thing to waste.")

- What were some of the bestselling songs and novels during your teen and young adult years?

The Political Factor

Julie, bragging as if the achievement were all hers, said at a fundraiser for a local candidate, "I was the first woman to be given a golf scholarship for college. It was after Title 9 was passed. It was a good thing because my dad was killed in Vietnam. With the benefits from the military and golf, I was able to finish my doctorate."

I (Bill) walked across the room to a group of men—former professional athletes. "Title 9 is the worst thing ever to happen to football. All these talented young men...and we have nothing to offer them because of the way the college interprets Title 9—giving an equal number of scholarships to women as to men. But football brings in all the money, and all the other sports use it up. That hardly seems fair." Political decisions do impact our futures.

On September 11, 2001, I (Pam) was set to speak at a seniors' luncheon. Early that morning, right after I had seen the horrific newscast of the planes flying into the Twin Towers in New York, my phone rang. It was Millie, the group's director. She was noticeably shaken, as were all the other seniors in the group. They had cancelled the day's events and were staying inside, each committing to pray. They didn't even want to venture out to pray together, as they were too frightened to be that far from home. Millie even said, "Oh! Pam, it's just like Pearl Harbor all over again!"

On the other end of the political spectrum are those who came of age during the Vietnam War. Many are either pro-military or radical peace protestors. Few people in that age range have no strong opinion one way or the other.

What are some questions you can ask to discover some of the political factors that might be contributing to someone's thoughts, words, or behaviors?

- What political persuasion were your parents?

- How active were your parents in politics?

- What do you see as the most important political moment of your lifetime?

- Which page of the newspaper do you read first? (Those influenced strongly by politics are apt to read the opinion page first.)

- Do you have any favorite political news shows? (If they have none, move on to other areas to gain more insights.)

- What do you think is the most important issue in the upcoming election?

The Media Factor

One day I felt as if I had television whiplash. Trina, my stylist, said, "Pam, we'll be moving to Oregon next month. I know it seems fast, but I just don't like the city anymore. I want a simpler life, so we're selling everything, and we bought 20 acres in the woods with a small cabin with a wood stove. It is going to be just like *The Waltons* or *Little House on the Prairie*." Then I went to a Tupperware party. There a woman was explaining her plans. "Yep, we're selling everything and moving to Miami. We bought a boat. It looks just like the one on *Miami Vice*—you know, the one Don Johnson lives on. That just seems so glamorous."

All my childhood friends wore the darling Dorothy Hamill haircut made popular after she won the Olympic gold medal for her ice-skating. Then they grew it out for the "Farrah" look, and then they all wanted to look like Jennifer Aniston of *Friend*s. Media definitely impacts the way we live.

After the release of the *Lord of the Rings* movies, the number of those taking fencing lessons rose dramatically. *Blair Witch Project* gave rise to a rekindled interest in the occult. Reality television gives everyone the illusion that they too can have their 15 minutes of fame, and perhaps they can—but at what cost? Eating worms for the camera, or having your heart broken by *The Bachelor*?

Mothers have a love-hate relationship with role models like Britney Spears, a Mouseketeer who now strips down to next to nothing to sing, "I'm not that innocent!" Or Jennifer Lopez, who is a sweet struggling single mother in the movie *Maid in Manhattan,* and then in her music video, *Jenny from the Bronx,* appears nude. What are these messages saying?

How will a generation be influenced by the longest-running sitcom, *Friends?* By the time *Friends* ends, the characters will have all had sex with one another. Is that really what friends do? One 19-year-old girl told me, "We don't really 'date,' we just kind of hang out as a group. I never even went out with Maxx. We just stayed at his place later than all the rest one time and I found myself in bed with him. But I'm not, like, in a relationship with him or anything." The influence of media?

The media powerfully influences all of us—for better or for worse. Technology can teach us much about our world. Television programs inform us about landscaping, art, history, transportation, architecture, and everything else imaginable. Movies provide great entertainment and memories to families as well as an industry full of productive careers. The media can promote the things you believe in and unify your circle of influence. But these influences can also erode the values you hold dear. They can expose your family to morals, ethics, and strategies you disapprove of in a captivating way. As a result, we must all create filters through which we allow sights and sounds to flow into our lives.

Here are a few questions to ask to find out what media impacts someone (and how much):

- How much television do you watch (including videos and DVDs)?

- How much time have you spent playing computer games?

- What is your favorite news show?

- What television shows were your favorites as a kid?

- Do you have a favorite movie? Why is it your favorite?

- Of all the commercials you have seen, which one sticks in your mind?

- Who is your favorite recording artist?

- What was the most popular song when you were in high school?

- What famous person do you admire and why?

The Ethnic Culture Factor

I love my friend Rosita. She is bright, well educated, friendly, and thoughtful. But every time I invite her anywhere, even to meet me for coffee, she doesn't simply reply, "I'll ask Jose," but rather, "I'll see if Jose will let me go."

When this first happened, my mind said, *Let you go? He's not your dad. He isn't your boss. He doesn't own you!* Then I went to her birthday party and met her entire extended family. All the women talked like that. All the women served the men first. All the women had traditional roles in the home: cooking, cleaning, and caring for children. When I mentioned that Bill ironed his shirt, I thought the world was going to stop turning. They were all in shock. The ethnic culture was definitely something I needed to consider to get to know my friend!

The Japanese are known for their politeness and their generous spirit. The German people are proud of their independence. Those in the southern United States are known for their hospitality, New Yorkers for their toughness. Jeresha, like many young women in the inner city, was expected to be pregnant by 14 and to be a single mother, so she was ridiculed for her tenacious and lofty goal of a college degree. Maria wore her father down with daily pleadings to be allowed to go away to college instead of working in the family business. Aman seemed so kind, so generous. He was always buying Janet beautiful things. He seemed to watch over her every need, but when she and the children went to live in his hometown in the Middle East, she was not allowed to go out of the house without a burka and without him. His care had turned to control. And the valedictorian at my son's high school was a young Asian woman who had not only over a 4.5 GPA but also 77 *college* units already completed.

Culture is definitely a factor in who we become. Breaking stereotypes is admirable, but ignoring culture and its influence on us and on our relationships is dangerous.

- Have you ever studied your family tree?

- What countries are your ancestors from?

- Do you have special foods or traditions in your family because of your culture?

- What would you say are the top three values in your cultural background?

- Are there any cultural taboos I would want to be aware of if I were a foreign exchange student to your country of origin?

- What are the typical roles for males and females in your cultural tradition?

The Educational Factor

We were sitting around the dinner table with friends. One of the men had earned a Ph.D. But he told us that he was a D student throughout most of elementary school. "In every grade, I was told to

'Sit down, be quiet. Why can't you act like Lisa? See how quietly she sits?' Every report card said I was a disruption. All the teachers wanted me on Ritalin. But bless my mom—she said, 'No, I'll help him learn to sit in his chair, and you help him learn once he is there.' In sixth grade I had two teachers—Mrs. Grayson, the mom of four sons, and Mr. Richardson. They discerned I was a kinetic learner and I needed to do something to retain the information. And because they understood boys, to them I wasn't a disruption but a student with a lot of drive and energy. So they put me to work in the classroom after I completed my assignments. I got straight As after that because I finally gained some confidence in the classroom."

How we are educated does impact our life. I (Pam) believe I never had a math teacher who could teach me math in a way I could learn it after third grade, so I have an aversion to math. Trying to combat it, I took a "Math for Women" course in college, where I learned that many women had these same feelings. When I was being educated, math was taught in a way that hindered most women from excelling, or they were not encouraged to excel.

Boys in the lower grades are often labeled as slow or uncooperative just because the developmental process for a boy is different from that of a girl. They need more large muscle movement, so sitting for long periods doesn't suit young males well. The coursework we are exposed to, the level at which we are expected to perform, and the attitude of our educators toward us all shape the way we see our intellectual selves and may also influence other areas of our self-concept. We have yet to elect a woman president, but the majority of college students are women. How has education impacted you and those you are in relation to? Here are a few questions to help you dig a little deeper into the heart of those you long to know more fully:

- What was your favorite subject as a child?

- Who was your favorite teacher? Why was he or she your favorite?

- Did you have any negative experiences in school?

- Do you think boys and girls were treated differently in your grade school? High school? College?

- Were you encouraged to take specific subjects and avoid others?

- What was your mother's education? Your dad's?

- What were your parents' opinions about education—especially college?

The Trauma Factor

Shelly was hard to draw out. She would never accept any of my invitations to an evening event. If she did say yes to a daytime event, she preferred I pick her up, and she always made up a reason for me to come in for a few minutes. One day over a cup of tea in her living room, I mentioned one more invitation to an evening women's event. This one was a self-defense class.

"Wow, this is a hard one," she mused. "Ummm...I usually don't go out at night. It's too scary for me. I was raped a couple years ago, and I am still pretty freaked out. But I was thinking maybe I would feel better if I took a tae kwon do class or something. I'll go if you pick me up."

Sandie had her life set: She earned a college degree, and she was set to marry her college sweetheart in a few months. The week before the wedding, her fiancé left town and left a note: "Sorry, just not ready for marriage." Several years later, Sandie began to date, but in her heart she always wondered if this guy would bail too.

Dave told Kayli while dating that she was not outgoing enough; Cindy told Todd, "You are too sensitive for a guy." People we trust betray us; people we love say things in the heat of an argument. A scar, a reminder is formed. It can affect our present relationship, the next relationship, or even several. Only as we take the hurt and pain to God can God repair the hole made by the trauma.

Trauma can range from relational setbacks to more severe experiences such as being a prisoner of war or surviving a bombing, a shooting, a robbery, or a rape. Real trauma may be caused by a gang rape, a beating that leaves you close to death, a car accident that leaves you permanently disabled, or an illness that changes the course of your life. Even a trauma in your family that didn't happen to you can alter the course of your life and the way you handle relationships. George W. Bush was the second-born son, but his older sibling died in childhood. George took on the role and character qualities of a firstborn leader. Our friend Shelly has a brother with Down syndrome, so she is hypersensitive to jokes or labels about people being dumb or stupid. Trauma can be an obstacle to overcome or a footstep into the future, depending on how you use the pain.

One woman I know had a mother who was married six times by the time my friend was 18. Her ability to trust men was almost nil until she received some intense counseling and did a several-year study of God as her Father. Donnie Dee, formerly a professional football player, shared a quote with me from a coach he had: "It is our pains that define us." The way we handle the worst days reveals our character, and our response to trauma builds our character. To truly know someone, you have to know about their darkest days, their deepest pains, and their rocky roads. Here are a few questions for deeper discovery.

- What was the most difficult day in your life?

- What do you think would be the hardest thing for a person to endure?

- Do you have any disappointments with life? With people?

- If you could live one day over and do it differently, what would you change and why?

The Religious Factor

"Pam, aren't you afraid to travel alone?" my friend Candace asked me. Candace seemed to have many fears. She always wore dresses and rarely wore makeup. She always asked me, "What do you think?" or "Is that right?" She was over 40 and had never driven out of our city alone. She had never spent the night away from her husband. One day over lunch I found out why. Candace had grown up in a religiously ultraconservative home. The wife's place was making babies or making dinner. Dad made all decisions—even what mom and all the daughters wore. Candace wasn't allowed to date until college. Her marriage was arranged between two families of her sect. She was never alone with her fiancé until their wedding night.

Religious upbringing can be either the greatest strength and foundation to a young life or the greatest source of pain and rebellion. One of my friends went to a Catholic school and excelled in that educational system. She had loving, dedicated parents who took their children to Mass and then home to a wonderful meal and an afternoon of fun with the extended family. She has a happy, stable marriage and has raised eight very successful children.

Another friend was molested by a priest and has tossed God out with the church. Still another friend clings to her belief in God but rejects the church of her youth because to her it represents a guilt-driven faith.

Philip Yancey, who has won numerous awards for his writing, penned a book called *Soul Survivor*, in which he recounted surviving the legalistic, narrow-minded, and even bigoted church of his youth. He has gone forward to be a leader in reconciliation between races and denominations.

How are we affected when people terrorize others in the name of God? How do we process the news of people like David Koresh of Waco, or Jim Jones, who brainwashed his followers and convinced them to drink poisoned Kool-Aid? How do we feel when we hear that a transient who claims to be anointed by God kidnaps Elizabeth Smart and holds her captive for months?

How can we have an authentic faith in God when most of us have never even read a holy book cover to cover to see for ourselves what is in it? Past generations saw the Bible as absolute truth, so they easily recognized injustice in the world. Most of the Ivy League schools were first seminaries or Bible colleges, but now those who claim a faith in God can be ridiculed in those same halls.

Consider the reformation movements: Catherine Booth of the Salvation Army led a movement to eradicate teen prostitution. Martin Luther King Jr. had a faith and a dream that stood up to racism. John Newton turned from trading slaves to trusting the Savior. He led the abolition movement in England and wrote one of the most beloved hymns of all time, *Amazing Grace.* How will we impact a generation in which most people do not believe in absolute truth?

If absolute truth doesn't exist, then what is wrong with extramarital affairs? Killing babies? Multiple sex partners? Incest? Rape? If it feels good, do it—right? *Wrong.* Even if you don't believe in absolute truth, that truth still exists. Many people today claim to be relativists, rejecting the notion of absolute truth. My friend Clay Jones who was president of a law school and hosted a national call-in radio program called *Contend for Truth,* lays out a pretty clear argument against relativism:

1. Relativism is the idea that there is no absolute moral truth.

   The relativist says something like, "You have your truth, and I have my truth. Your truth is no better than my truth, my truth is no better than your truth, and there is no truth with a capital 'T.'" The relativist believes, therefore, that every philosophy or religion is equal in value and all are equally respectable. There are several problems with the concept of relativism. Despite the problems with this concept, four out of five people now hold to it.

2. Relativism is self-refuting because saying "there is no absolute truth" is making an absolute statement.

   That statement is an absolute statement about moral truth, and so it is self-refuting. There is also a contradiction in the relativist's thought because when he or she argues for tolerance, he or she is presupposing there is actual right and wrong.

3. Relativism condones even the most horrific evils, such as the Nazi genocide or torturing babies for fun.

    Relativists are absolutely incapable of unequivocally condemning even the greatest horrors. After all, if one person's truth is no better than another person's truth, then you cannot begin to condemn any philosophy whatsoever. Take the Taliban. We may respect them as persons, but can we respect a philosophy advocating that women should be shot for not wearing burkas and that women should not see a doctor? Of course not. Was the Nazi final solution something we should respect? Should we not unequivocally condemn it? Of course we should. To the uninformed, relativism may look like the best way to prevent racism, but, when held consistently, it actually becomes the racist's friend.

4. Relativism is utterly hypocritical because relativists really only tolerate other relativists.

    Relativism's claim to fame is that it is tolerant of other religions and philosophies. It is not. The only people that relativists tolerate are other relativists. People who hold that their religion is absolutely true are often strenuously opposed by the relativist. Only those adherents of various religions or philosophies who share the relativist's perspective on reality—that their religion or philosophy is no better than anyone else's—are truly welcome.[3]

The relativist chooses his or her belief system and the attitude that says, "Whatever, Dude!" We make our choices and our choices make us. The negative consequences of relative thinking will play out whether you believe they will or not. Truth exists whether you believe it does or not.

Aligning your life and choices with truth would seem like common sense. But people have a hard time thinking their way to truth. George Barna gathered some statistics about faith in America that send mixed signals.

> A new study of how American adults view themselves finds those associated with the Christian faith are more likely than others to claim traditional values and to be concerned about the nation's moral condition; atheists, agnostics and people associated with non-Christian faiths are most likely to be politically liberal *and least likely to say they are happy;* and *evangelicals are the most conservative, most satisfied, most spiritually inclined and least stressed out of all U.S. adults.*[4]

However, only 8 percent of Americans classify themselves as evangelicals.[5] You'd think, based upon the fact that a high of *99 percent of evangelicals describe themselves as happy,* more people would be clamoring to become evangelical in their beliefs. Though 72 percent believe that God is the all-powerful, all-knowing, perfect Creator that rules the world today, the 2002 data showed that church attendance was only 43 percent of all adults in a typical week. Attendance spiked after the September 11 terrorist attacks, but within a few weeks of the attacks, the attendance levels returned to normal. In total, fewer than one out of three adults in America attend church with consistency. Only half of the adults who say they are Christians contend that they are "absolutely committed" to the Christian faith. Though 60 percent of all adults agree that "the Bible is totally accurate in all of its teachings, only 39 percent of Americans read the Bible each week outside of church.[6] *We want to be happy, but we don't want to do the things that will get us there!*

When asked what he found to be most surprising about the data, George Barna replied, "Perhaps the paradox of living in a culture defined by constant change, with a nation of people who admit to confusion regarding purpose, meaning and truth, and yet finding that there has been no real change in the spiritual views and endeavors of the people."[7]

So what do those people who describe themselves as evangelical believe? Why do 99 percent of them describe themselves as "happy," while such a slim percentage of the rest of the world would even come close to describing themselves as happy? What makes evangelicals so happy?

Evangelicals are a subset of the born-again population. We believe that born-again people are those who have prayed a prayer to God that would include these tenets (the words themselves can be expressed in a variety of ways):

> God, I believe Your Word, the Bible, is Truth. I believe You are the all-knowing, all-powerful, perfect Deity who created the universe and still rules it today. I believe I am imperfect, sinful. I believe You, God, came down to earth because You loved me. You, Jesus, are God, and You are sinless, so only You could pay the penalty for my sin. You died on the cross because You loved me. I can't work my way to You, so I accept that free gift of love. I see the evil in the world. I believe Satan does exist. I reject Satan and evil, and I choose You, God. I am so grateful, thankful, and excited about Your love for me that I want to share that love with others, not because I have to but because I want to. Amen.

Yes, we make our choices and our choices make us. What's your choice?

Deliberate choices leave lasting results. I was able to see an amazing example of this recently. Visiting a small conference grounds in Darmstadt, Germany, I learned the amazing story behind this Protestant nunnery.

A group of young German women had been living in a religious sect in a small farmhouse when Hitler was rising in power. They discerned the evil in Hitler's heart and began to pray that God would deliver Germany from his grip. These young women prayed to find land on which to build a retreat center where people from all over the world could come to hear about and experience God's love. In answer to their prayers, a farmer donated some land. But they had nothing to build with and no money, so they continued to pray.

One dear sister was out walking when the mayor of the town stopped and asked her if she wanted a ride. When he heard of their desire to build a retreat center, he told them about some German military barracks being torn down. He asked, "Would you like the bricks?" The young women walked back and forth—six miles each way—carrying the blocks in their aprons. The women built a chapel, a home, a beautiful garden, and eventually a retreat center.

This is a picture of many factors at work: an authentic faith in God, a unique political climate, the need for social change, and a desire to live out relationships based on love. The depravity and selfishness of one generation can lead to brokenness, repentance, and a revival. A new generation that is sick of hypocrisy, selfish living, and people using people can lift up a standard of truth. *We make our choices and our choices make us.*

Religion can have a positive influence on a life, but a *relationship* with God can have an amazing impact! Here are some questions you can discuss with those you'd like to understand more completely.

- Tell about your religious journey.

- What do you remember thinking or feeling about God when you were a child?

- What are the spiritually significant moments of your life?

- How active was your family in a local church?

- What were your holiday celebrations like? Which were most important, and how did you celebrate them?

- What were your Sabbath or weekly holy days like?

- Who were some of your spiritual mentors and role models?

- Did you attend parochial or religious school?

- What is faith in God to you? What do you base your faith on?

- Explain how you think a person of faith's life should look. What exemplifies a person who loves God? What is his or her life like?

In an article in *Time* magazine entitled, "What Makes You Who You Are" (June 2, 2003), Matt Ridley sums up the latest research in the age-old nature vs. nurture argument:

> In this new view, genes allow the human mind to learn, remember, imitate, imprint language, and absorb culture and express instincts. Genes are not puppet masters or blueprints, nor are they just carriers of heredity. They are active during life; they switch one another on and off, they respond to the environment. They may direct the construction of the body and brain in the womb, but then almost at once in response to experience, they set about dismantling and rebuilding what they have made. They are both the cause and the consequence of our actions.

God sets certain traits and characteristics in our DNA. Then our environment influences us, but we choose how to use all the pieces of the puzzle. As we learn more about ourselves, as we acknowledge all the factors that go into making up a person, we learn to improve our relational skills. People are drawn to us because we are able to relate, give empathy, and understand. When we consider the many complex issues that make up a person, we are more likely to be able to help people reach their God-given potential. We can see that our environment influences us, but it does not have to define us or our future. We learn tools to help us overcome obstacles and turn them into opportunities. The opportunity to make the most of your relationships is now yours. *We make our choices, and our choices make us.* What are you choosing?

Why Did You Do That?

1. Which of these influence your relationships the most?

   - communication
   - parents
   - economics
   - society
   - family
   - friends
   - politics
   - media
   - ethnicity
   - education
   - trauma
   - religion

2. Have you been using any of these factors for an excuse not to do or to be your best?

3. How did this chapter help you better understand yourself?

4. How can what you learned help you in a work or social relationship?

5. With all of these variables, our differences could potentially splinter any group or movement. How can the information in this chapter be used to build unity rather than division?

Notes

Chapter 1—Why Did You Do That?

1. Bill and Pam Farrel, *Men Are Like Waffles, Women Are Like Spaghetti* (Eugene, OR: Harvest House Publishers, 2001), 11-14.

2. Simon LeVay, *The Sexual Brain* (Cambridge, MA: The MIT Press, 1993), 21.

3. The statistics cited in this section are from Margaret Matlin, *The Psychology of Women* (New York: Holt, Rinehart and Winston, 1987), 38-59.

4. James Dobson, *Bringing Up Boys* (Wheaton, IL: Tyndale House Publishers, 2001), 16.

Chapter 2—The Male and Female Brains

1. Simon LeVay, *The Sexual Brain* (Cambridge, MA: The MIT Press, 1993), 26.

2. Ibid.

3. Ibid., 87.

4. Ibid., 77.

5. Ibid., 101.

6. Ibid., 102-03.

7. Kristin Cobb, "His-and-Her Hunger Pangs," *Science News* vol. 162, no. 1, July 6, 2002, 4.

8. Malcolm Ritter, "Brains Differ in Navigation Skills," AP, March 21, 2000. © Copyright 2000 The Associated Press. (Found at list.k12.ar.us/pipermail/science/2000-March/ 000225.html)

9. Phil McGraw, "Dr. Phil's Man-ual," *O, The Oprah Magazine,* June 2003, 47.

10. Transcribed from September 4, 2001 ABC interview with Barbara Walters. (www.abcnews.go.com/sections/2020/2020/2020_010904_heche2.html)

11. Simon LeVay, *The Sexual Brain* (Cambridge, MA: The MIT Press, 1993), 98.

12. Daniel J. Canary and Tara M. Emmers-Sommer with Sandra Faulkner, *Sex and Gender Differences in Personal Relationships* (New York: The Guilford Press, 1997), 30.

13. Ibid., 31.

14. Jennifer Warner, "Scientists Learn to Mimic Brain's 'All-Clear' Signal," WebMD Medical News, November 6, 2002. (my.webmd.com/content/article/53/61393.htm)

15. Jennifer Warner, "Scream for a Healthy Heart," WebMD Medical News, November 6, 2002. (my.webmd.com/content/article/60/67095.htm)

Chapter 3—Physical Differences

1. John Nicholson, *Men and Women: How Different Are They?* (Oxford: Oxford University Press, 1984), 28-29.

2. Ibid., 45.

3. Ibid., 46.

4. Ibid.

5. Ibid., 48.

6. Ibid., 49.

7. Deborah Holtzman, et al., "State- and Sex-Specific Prevalence of Selected Characteristics —Behavioral Risk Factor Surveillance System, 1996 and 1997," *Morbidity and Mortality Weekly Report.* (www.cdc.gov/mmwr/preview/mmwrhtml/ss4906a1.htm)

Chapter 5—The Waffle Warrior

1. Quoted in Alan Webber, "Why Can't We Get Anything Done?" *Fast Company,* June 2000, 168.

2. John Eldredge, *Wild at Heart* (Nashville: Thomas Nelson Publishers, 2001), 3-5.

3. John Nicholson, *Men and Women: How Different Are They?* (Oxford: Oxford University Press, 1984), 160.

4. Ibid., 160-61.

5. Ibid., 161.

6. Reported in "Ball Games Raise Testosterone Levels," Science a GoGo, May 19, 1998. (www.scienceagogo.com/news/19980419140959data_trunc_sys.shtml)

7. Nicholson, *Men and Women,* 170.

8. I (Bill) will always be indebted to John Eldredge for expressing this theme throughout *Wild at Heart.*

9. Nancy Ammon Jianakoplos and Alexandra Bernasek, "Are Women More Risk Averse?" *Economic Inquiry,* vol. 36, no. 4, October 1998, 620-30.

10. Ibid.